WORKING STATUS OF CHILD WORKER

Provisions and Prohibitions

WORKING STATUS OF CHILD WORKER

Provisions and Prohibitions

By
Dr. Aditya Kumar Patra
Deptt. of Economics
Kalinga Mahavidyalaya
Berhampur University
G.Udayagiri, Kandhamal Distt.
(Orissa)

DISCOVERY PUBLISHING HOUSE PVT. LTD.
NEW DELHI-110 002

First Published-2010

ISBN 978-81-8356-647-6

Published by:

DISCOVERY PUBLISHING HOUSE PVT. LTD.
4831/24, Ansari Road, Prahlad Street
Darya Ganj, New Delhi-110002 (India)
Phone: 23279245, 43764432 • Fax: 91-11-23253475
E-mail: parul.wasan@gmail.com
info@discoverypublishinggroup.com
Website: www.discoverypublishinggroup.com

Printed at:
Sachin Printers
Delhi

Preface

Children are the budding resources and the future citizen of a nation. Child development is considered as a prerequisite for national development. Unfortunately, child labour is widespread and has emerged as a burning issue in our country. Though, child labour is found in all regions of the world, it is overwhelming phenomenon in a developing country, concentrated in rural area and biased against boys. It is universally condemned as an intolerable disrespect for human dignity and an enormous waste of human resources. Child labour persists nonetheless. There is no single determining cause for the prevalence of child labour. The cause for child labour is a multi-dimensional one: Economic, Socio-Cultural, Political and Administrative, Legal and Employer Friendly factors. Physical, cognitive, emotional, social and moral developments of child are endangered on account of the menace of child labour.

The International Labour Organisation (ILO) and the Government of India have adopted concentrated effort to eliminate the problem of child labour. Along with the constitutional safeguards, several regulating Acts have been enacted and various projects have been initiated at different points of time by the Government of India, yet this man-made disaster continues with its ugly face.

An empirical investigation has been attempted in this report to study the problem of child labour in the district of Kandhamal, a tribal pocket of Orissa. The study shows that the incidence of child labour declines over time in Kandhamal district. It is a welcome sign. However, it is not due to persuasion of any specific programme designed towards this end, rather on account of increase of social awareness of the parents and the people in general. Laws alone cannot solve the problem. A multi-pronged attack is indispensable. Public awareness along with local capacity building and an improvement of the legal and organizational environment is essential. Best result can be obtained if several actors: Government, Parents and Employers work together.

"Let's arm our children with opportunity and hope.
Our slogan is 'parents to work and children to school."

Aditya Kumar Patra

Abbreviations

AITUC	:	All-India Trade Union Congress
AMCS	:	Agency Marketing Cooperative Society
CITU	:	Centre of Indian Trade Union
CLASP	:	Child Labour Action Support Programme
HMS	:	Hindu Mazdoor Sabha
ILO	:	International Labour Organisation
IPEC	:	International Programme for the Elimination of Child Labour
NAECL	:	National Authority for the Elimination of Child Labour
NCLP	:	National Child Labour Project
NGO	:	Non-Government Organisations
NRCCL	:	National Resource Centre on Child Labour
NSSO	:	National Sample Survey Organisation
RMCS	:	Regulated Market Committee Society
SIMPCO	:	Statistical Information and Monitoring Programme on Child Labour
TDCC	:	Tribal Development Credit Co-operatives
UNDP	:	United Nations Development Programme
UNICEF	:	United Nations International Children's Emergency Fund
VVGNLI	:	V.V.Giri National Labour Institute

Contents

1
Introduction

India is often described as "the largest democracy in the world". Largest it certainly is. It has a credible electoral system, an independent judiciary, a free press, vibrant social movement, a strong argumentative tradition and so on. But unfortunately the well-being and rights of children count less. The glaring example is the failure to deliver on the 86th Amendment of the Constitution of India, which made education as a fundamental right for all children aged 6-14 years. Indeed, poor children are twice removed from the center of attention: not only do they belong to the families that have little voice in the political system; they also have no voice within the family.

Children are the budding resources and the future citizen of a nation. The future of a nation lies in the proper nourishment of its children. A healthy and educated child of today is the active and intelligent citizen of tomorrow. Hence, it is pertinent to look into various aspects of this important segment of human resources. The UNDP's Human Development Report 1996 proclaims that the children, who should have been most protected in any society, are indeed subject to many abuses like neglect, malnutrition, deficiency of food, underweight, mental-retardation, etc. Another astounding problem of children is the evil of child labour.

Child labour is the work which involves some degree of exploitation, i.e., physical, mental, psychological and economic. Therefore, it impairs the health and development of children. Statistical Information and Monitoring Programme on Child Labour (SIMPOC) applies the term 'working children' to economically active children. "This concept is so broad as to encompass most production activities undertaken by children, whether for the market or not, paid or unpaid, part time or full time, on a casual basis or a regular one, in the formal sector or the informal, whether the activities are legal or illegal". Child labour is a subset of this group.

The major factors responsible for the growth of child labour are poverty, rapid population growth, deterioration in living standard and the incapacity of education system to cater to all children of school going age and provide them with a decent education.

Some 250 million children between the ages of 5 and 14 are working in developing countries. Of this total some 120 million children are working full-time and 130 million works part-time.[1]

Although the internationally recommended minimum age for work is 15 year (ILO convention – No 38), almost all the data available on child labour concern the 10-14 age group. ILO estimated that more than 73 million children of the age group 10-14 were economically active in 1995, which represent 30.2 per cent of all in the world. The greatest number are found in Asia - 44.6 million i.e., 13 per cent followed by Africa - 23.6 million 26.3 per cent. Estimate by country shows that in India 14.4 per cent of the total children in the age group 10-14 are engaged in economic activities.[2]

But this is only a part of the whole picture. As mentioned by ILO no reliable figures on worker under 10 are available though their numbers we know, are significant. It is true of children between 14 and 15 on whom few report exist. If all of these could be counted and if proper accounts are taken of the domestic work performed full-time by girls, a total number of child workers around the world today might well be in hundreds of million.

While child labour is found in all region of the world, it is overwhelmingly a developing country phenomenon. It is mostly found in rural sector, with as many as 17 per cent of all child labourers involved in agriculture activities. Available statistics suggest that more boys than girls are working as child labour.

Children have only one childhood; childhood is a period of life which should be devoted not to work but to education and development. Child labours very often destroy children's chance of a potential and productive future. Being forced to work too early in life may cripple children physically and mentally.

Ever since the establishment of International Labour Organization (ILO) 1919, it has adopted a concentrated effort to eliminate child labour but this man-made disaster continues with its ugly face. Immediately after its establishment ILO adopted a convention prohibiting work of children below 14 years of age in industrial undertakings. ILO strives hard to give a decent childhood to every body. With the launching of the International Program for the Elimination of Child Labour (IPEC) 1992-93, ILO embarks on a course of action to put an end to this scandal. India is the first country to sign MOU with ILO in 1992. On 12th June of every year the world-day against child labour is observed in every corner of the Globe. This year a month-long campaign has been observed in India to eliminate child labour in the match and firework industry as a part of IPEC activity.[3]

Article 24 of the Indian Constitution prohibits employment of children below the age of 14 year in factories, mines and hazardous works. In addition, two directive principle of the States policy under Articles 39(e) and (f) and Article 45 stipulate that the State must prevent children from being forced by economic necessity to enter vocations unsuited to their health and strength. It further states that childhood and youth should be protected against exploitations and mental deteriorations. The Government of India has passed a good number of legislations to tackle the problem of child labour. The child labour prohibition and regulation Act 1986 is the latest in this row. Government started National Child Labour Project (NCLP) and set up the Nationl Authority for the Elimination of Child labour (NAECL) in 1994. A child Labour Technical Advisory Committee has also been set up for recommending action plans and programmes.

In spit of these efforts child labour persists in India. It is very unfortunate to mention that as per 2001 census there are 1.25 crore working children in the age group of 5 to 14 years as compared to the total child population of 25.2 crore. This is nothing but to say that out of the total child population 5.9 per cent are working children.[4]

The survey conducted by the labour commission orissa 1997 shows that in orissa out of the total 2,15,222 child labour identified male constitutes 56.5 per cent where as female are a little low i.e., 43.5 per cent. So far as activities are concerned 88.9 per cent child labour are engaged in non-hazardous activities.[5] The survey reveals that in Kandhmal district about 4.9 per cent of the total child population is engaged as child labour. Out of 6456 child labourers identified 3376 are boys and 3080 are girls. All the child labourers are engaged in non-hazardous activities such as Agriculture, domestic service, trading activities and collection of forest product, etc.

The Government of India takes several steps to solve the problem of child labour by establishing National Child Labour Projects in different States. The package of service under National Child Labour Project includes special schools to provide non-formal education vocational training supplementary nutrition, stipend, health care etc. Concrete efforts towards elimination of this child labour population are being planned to be taken up in the Xth plan to eliminate child labour in a convergent and time bound manner.

Review of Literature

The International Labour Organisation (ILO) and United Nations International Children's Emergency Fund (UNICEF) have produced a large number of literatures on child labour at international level. A few of them have been briefed below.

The ILO in its "Child Work, Poverty and Under Development" (1981) has focused on determinants and consequence of child labour problem. In "Action Against Child Labour" (2000) edited by Nelien Haspels and Michele Jankanish for ILO, the vital functions of national policies and programmes against child labour have been examined with reference to Thailand, Tanzania, Philippines, India, Pakistan, Nepal and Bangladesh.

Elias Mendelievich (1979)[6] has dealt with child labour in a broader perspective for ILO. The work is based on an international survey of child labour in 11 countries. He analyzed the laws, causes, working conditions and consequence of child labour in these nations. The study concluded that developing and less developed nations have maximum incidence of child labour. The principal causes for child labour in these nations are poverty, entrenched traditions and lack of infrastructure facilities. Contrary to this in developed nations the child labour occurred only in agriculture sector as extra hands needed during sowing and harvesting seasons.

Gerry Rodgers and G.Standing (1981)[7] assessed the role of working children in low income countries. The study is based on macro data at national level culled from ILO bureau of statistics on child labour. The key issue of the study was to know the extent of exploitation of these children in socio-economic context. They commented that suppression of child labour is unlikely to increase the welfare of the child, where substitute income sources are absent. Hence, there is need to increase the welfare of such children that would gradually eliminate this evil.

Lee Swepston's study (1982)[8] pointed out that in spite of the recognition of child labour as being undesirable, harmful, it still persists because of poverty and underdevelopment. He has examined regulation standards of ILO and other national legislations to combat child labour *vis-à-vis* its existence. He concludes that the approach of setting minimum ages of work will not abolish the problem of child labour rather an all round development and understanding of the problem of low income will only help to control the child labour. The abolition of child labour will be a gradual process and will take its own time to vanish.

UNICEF's publication "Implementation Hand Book for the Convention on the Rights of the Child" (1998) provides a reference for the implementation of law, policy and practice to promote and protect the rights of children.

Learning and Working (1995) is a compailation of works on child labour and basic education by the UNICEF. In this study the situation of child labour in Ghana, Nigeria, Peru, India, USA and Colombia has been described. The study argues necessity of compulsory education for elimination of child labour.

Studies have also been made at national and state level. A few of them have been focused below.

Before seventies three important commissions were set up by the Government of India to study the problem of labour in all sectors. These are Royal Commission of Labour (Whitily Commission, 1931), the Labour Investigation Commission (Rege Commission, 1945) and the National Commission on Labour (Justice P.V Ganjendra Ghadkar commission). The commissions had studied the problem of child labour and recommended a good number of suggestions. The present legislations for child labour are mainly based on these recommendations.

The Government of India in its maiden official report of post-Independent era (1954) vividly analyzed the different aspects of child labour, viz. the extent, wages, hours of work, working conditions and health status of child labour. The report mentions the legislative protection taken by the government for children. The report also examines the correlation between lack of opportunity of elementary education and proliferation of child labour.

Kulshrestha (1978) analyzed the plight of child labour in unorganized sector along with legislative provision to tackle the problem. He has attributed the causes of child labour, inter alia, to low wages of the adults, unemployment of the adult workers, lack of social security schemes for poor families, large family size, rural-urban migration, low literacy rate and absence of compulsory education. He elaborately deals with the legal provisions extended to Indian children and confesses their futility. He praises the roles of voluntary organizations in creating awareness about the evils of child labour and securing social justice for them.[9]

The National Institution of Public Co-operation and Child Development, New Delhi, conducted a detailed survey on working children engaged in informal sectors of Mumbai Metro (1978).

Pramila Pandit Barooah (1978) has studied the problem of child labour of Delhi engaged in organized and unorganized segment of primary and secondary sectors.[10]

K.C. Seal (1979), discussed the basic facts about girl child labour and reason for it. He concluded that labour deprives the child of his education and prevents proper development of his potential.[11]

M. Patnaik (1979) in agreement with K.C.Seal in her work "Child labour in India" derived same conclusions. These conclusions were based on correlation between incidence of child labour and low level of literacy.[12]

S.N. Jain (1979) has highlighted the problem of child labour and discussed the existing laws enacted by the Government to handle the situation.[13]

The Gurupada Swami Committee (1979) has brought to light the living condition of child labour in different parts of Indian sub-continent particularly in unorganized hazardous activities.[14]

'Child Labour: A Threat to Health and Development' is an edited volume (1981) includes a good number of articles related to different aspects of child labour. It contains empirical studies on exploitation of child labour in Asia and Africa. A study on the impact of child labour on health condition of the child in Indian sub-continent is also examined in the volume.[15]

Juyal (1985) has examined the inhuman exploitation inflicted upon child labours in the Bilwaria area of Maharashtra.[16]

B.M.Dinesh in his 'Economic Activities of Children: Dimensions, Causes and Consequences' (1988)[17] deals with the economic contribution of children and the back-ground causes of child labour in Karnataka. The study presents a virtuous trend on the basis of data collected from 1971 and 1981 census. According to him, incentives to reduce the fertility rate would bring down the incidence of child labour.

Jha (1989) has examined the causes of child labour and suggests few policy recommendations. He has the opinion that the best way to attack the menace of child labour is to ensure that every child should be enrolled in the school. To him the crux of the problem is the effective implementation of labour laws. The enforcement machinery is woefully inadequate and in the unorganized sector, it becomes even more acute.[18]

Tripathy (1989)[19] studied the problems of bonded labour in Indian state with special reference to Orissa. This study has pointed out the tribal indebtedness and bondage leading to distress living condition of children. Absence of employment in rural area, failure of crops, poverty, and indebtedness are the vital factors of migration of child labour.[20] His analysis of laws and legislations drew conclusion that, there should be no minimum age limit to enter labour force. In fact, author proposed total ban on employing children below the age of 14 years and extends this ban to maximum possible industries.

Alec Fyfe (1989)[21] examined in detail the anatomy and consequence of child labour and concluded that child labour of rural and urban sector differ in their nature of work and amount of exploitation. Urban child labourers are exploited more than their rural counter parts. Reasons advocated are, in rural areas the children are working with their family. On the contrary urban child labourers work outside the family. Latters are exposed to urbanized hazards such as street children, scavenger, juvenile delinquency and debt bondage.

In a case study undertaken to examine the ill treatment given to the children employed in the canteens of educational institutions in south Delhi, Dr Benjamin (1990) concluded that poverty is the main cause of early employment. Despite their willingness, many parents find it difficult to educate their children because of lack of income and infrastructural facilities. These children have always a feeling of insecurity of their Jobs and that is why they are more submissive and easily exploited by their employers who kept them under the non-contractual recruitment arrangements. The boys work for prolonged hours per day with a little pay. They have almost lost their hopes for coming up in their life.[22]

B.K.Sharma *et al* (1990)[23] focused on the role of child labour in the urban informal sector. The impact of socio-economic background on conditions and attitude on child labour was studied. They were denied formal as well as informal education and male children were generally found to be working as labourers. However, in Sivakasi match industry girl children were inducted in to labour force mainly to allow their brothers to study at their cost.

Myron Weiner in his book *The Child and the State in India* (1991)[24] critically examined the problem of child labour vis-à-vis the education system in India. By examining the situation of 19th century Europe he rejects the argument that for removal of child labour in India, income of the poor should rise and the employers be in need of a more skilled labour force. To him the causes of child labour in India are deep rooted in the culture and her policies to combat child labour are designed on the basis of fundamental beliefs. He has drawn a pessimistic conclusion stating that "with illiteracy and child labour declining world wide at a faster rate than in India, India's global share of illiterates and child labourers will continue to increase".

Panicher and Nangia (1992) has examined on the living condition of migrated working street children of Delhi.[25]

Panday (1993) analysed the street children of Kanpur city. The nature extent of the problem of the street children and the family and environment in which they are living, the basic identified crisis etc. He also suggested certain policy initiatives to solve the problem.[26]

Vimal Farooqui (1994) Studied and analyses the census data 1981 and 1991 and discussed on the issue that being a girl, she is in a disadvantageous situation in our country from the birth, working girls are subjected to cruel treatment and sexual abuse. He stressed on the need for social awakening towards the status of women in general and girl child labour in particular. [27]

Verma and Jain (1995) have highlighted the role of All India Trade Union Congress (AITUC), the Center of Indian Tread Union (CITU), and the Hindu Mazdoor Sabha (HMS) in eradicating child labour in some specific trades.[28]

Dr Sahoo's study (1995) illuminates the factor and condition of child labour in two villages under changing agrarian production process.[29]

Farida Saha in her 'Scheduled Tribe Child Labour' (1996) outlines that the incidence of child labour gives a fatal blow on the human resource development programmes. The study highlights that child labour problem is high where poverty and illiteracy is rampant and it is an economic necessity in case of tribal children. Hence, for elimination of child labour a proper understanding and evaluation of various aspects of the problem is essential.

Anandharajakumar (1997) has studied the causes, consequences, the constitutional and extra constitutional provisions to tackle the problem of child labour in a greater detail. He has the opinion that the problem can be solved only when the attitude and morality of parents, exploiters and society at large get changed drastically in favour of children.[30]

Neera Burra (1997) carried out a field investigation in brassware factories (Uttar Pradesh), gem polishing factories (Rajasthan), lock making and glass factories (Uttar Pradesh), diamond cutting factories (Gujarat) in India. The findings of the investigation have been compiled in 'Born to Work: Child Labour in India' (1997).[31] There, Nerra Burra has documented the tragic plight of child labour. The working conditions of these children are full of tortures and abuses, which stunt the physical and mental growth; the sufferings of these children have been identified and narrated throughout the pages. The common conclusion drawn from all industries, poverty is the main cause for prevalence of child labour. The free and compulsory primary education will help in elimination of the evil. It was also suggested that there should be total ban on employment of children below the age of 14 years, rather than drawing distinction between hazardous and non-hazardous industries and varying the age of employment. This variation creates loopholes for the employment against the laws.

Rao (1998) studied the general profile of the female workers in beedi industry at macro-level in India. The earnings of female workers engaged in beedi industry are meagre so they involve their female children to work along with them to supplement their income. The leading states are West Bengal, Kerela, Karnataka and Tamil Nadu. The Beedi workers are exposed to dust, nicotine causing respiratory diseases and infertility in young women and girls.[32]

Investigations into the conditions of working children in the match industry of Sivakasi (Smita Kothari, 1998) and in the pencil factories of Madhya Pradesh (Nirmal Mitra, 1998) are some of the empirical analysis of the problem.

Rachita Jawa (1999) discussed the female child labour with reference to poverty at micro level. It was concluded that poverty, population and illiteracy each breed the other. The families having female children living below poverty line were first to put into the labour force. Poverty reduction, welfare oriented programmes, motivation of parents to educate their children, etc., can help the elimination of female child labour. [33]

Bimal Kumar in 'Problems of Working Children' (2000)[34] studied the problems of working children in lock making industries of Aligarh and brass ware industries of Moradabad. He finds that selective ban pushes the child labour from organized to semi-organised sector and than to un-organised sector, from respectable to less respectable type of work. So, he prescribes that programme should be launched to ban child labour in all occupations. Simultaneously, income augmenting schemes should be started covering cent per cent of the working children. Only such approach would be effective for imposition of ban on child labour.

Vijay Khare (2002) has analyzed the cause of child labour and reached the conclusion that "without a class less society India will not able to solve the social and economic problem of child labour".[35]

Nanjunda (2005) has the opinion that after the 73rd amendment of Indian Constitution Panchayat Raj Institutions have become important instruments for social and economic development at grass root level. Hence, PRI institutions should strive hard for elimination of child labour from rural belt of India.[36]

At this juncture, a time has come to analyze the problems with broad vision and to suggest suitable measure for their elimination. Against this literary backdrop a micro-level study is here undertaken to know the geneses of the problem, socio-economic impact of this evil practices on the society and measures taken by the government to tackle the problem. The conclusions drawn form this microanalysis may be extended with a macro-perspective to give a meaningful solution to this manmade disaster.

Objectives of the Study

The overall objective of this study is to understand socio-economic causes and consequences of child labour in Kandhamal district. Specific objectives of the study are enumerated below :

1. To analyse the genesis of the problem of child labour.
2. To out-line the dimension of the problem particularly in unorganized and informal sector of the Kandhamal district.
3. To study the schooling status of the children by the educational and economic position of the parents.
4. To study the nature of work activities and time spent on them.
5. The study endeavours to search possible solutions to the problem of child labour and a plan of action for prevention / elimination of child labour.

The study is exploratory and descriptive. It seeks to explore the facts regarding:

1. The causes and consequences of the problem.
2. Existing legislative measures and Acts and their efficacy to combat the problem of child labour.
3. The part played by NGOs administrators and General public to create awareness for the solution of this age-old problem.

Methodology

Keeping in view the objectives set forth earlier, it has been decided to collect information from both primary and secondary sources. For the collection of primary data a multi-stage random sampling method is followed. At the first stage out of 12 blocks and two urban areas the investigator selects 4 blocks and two urban areas namely Phulbani NAC and G.udayagiri NAC and G.udayagiri, Tikabali, Raikia and Chakapad block purposively. In the second stage from each block three villages / panchayatas are randomly selected for study. So, all together the investigator selects 12 villages/panchayatas and two urban centers for collection of data. In the third stage 10 child labourers of each center has been chosen on a simple random sampling basis as the primary unit of data collection.

Primary data were collected through personal interview method with the help of a structured questionnaire after pre-testing the questionnaire.

The first section of the questionnaire deals with the personal trait of the child labour, hence answers were collected from the child labor himself / herself. The second section pertains to the socio-economic background of the family of the child-labour, therefore answers ware collected from the parents/family members of the child labour.

The above data have been supplemented by secondary information gathered from official records, personal discussion with officials and field observations of the works undertaken in the sample villages/urban centers, relevant to the study were recorded in the form of field notes which became fruitful in drawing some meaningful inferences.

However, all efforts have been made to make the study just, appropriate and genuine so on to generalize the findings for the district as well as the state.

Hypotheses

To examine the problem stated in the earlier paragraph, the following hypotheses are considered in the study :

1. Poverty, lack of awareness and low level of living standard are the main causes of child labour in Kandhamal district.
2. A major part of child labour is engaged in trading and commercial activities.
3. The tender child labourers are very often ill treated by their employers.
4. Inaction of the government machinery is mainly responsible for the perpetuation of this problem.

After the hypotheses are set up, the study plans to examine the validity of these hypotheses with the help of an exploratory analysis.

Plan of the Study

The study is divided into five chapters.

Chapter 1 introduces the topic, outlines the scope and defines the methodology.

Chapter 2 deals with the concept of child labour from its historical background to contemporary situation. The Socio-economic and psychological reasoning for its continuation.

Chapter 3 is a review of statutory laws and constitutional safeguards outlined for prohibition of this evil practice in India.

Chapter 4 constitutes the hard core of the study. In this chapter all the primary and secondary data collected in the process has been analysed in a greater detail to have a better insight into the problem.

Chapter 5 presents a brief summary and conclusions derived from the study. It also prescribes few policy suggestions.

REFERENCES

1. *Child Labour: Targeting the Intolerable. International Labour Conference* (Report VI, i)-86th Session, 1998, ILO, Geneva.
2. *World of Work* No 16, 1996, pp. 12-13.
3. *World of Work* No 4, 1993, pp. 4-5.
4. *Economic Survey, 2004-05*, Government of India, New Delhi.
5. *Labour Statistics in Orissa, 2004*, Labour Commissioner, Government of Orissa, Bhubaneswar.
6. Mendelievich, Elias, 1979, Child Labour, *International Labour Review*, 118, 5, pp. 557-568
7. Rodgers, G. and Standing, G., 1981, Economic Roles of Children in low income Countries, *International Labour Review*, 120, 1.
8. Swepston, Lee, 1982, Child Labour: Its Regulations by ILO Standards and National Legislation, *International Labour Review*, 121, pp. 557-589
9. Kulshreshtha, J.C., 1978, *Child Labour in India*, Ashish Publishing House, New Delhi.

10. Peoples Union of Democracy, AIR, 1982, S.C., 1473.
11. Seal, K.C., 1979: 'Children and Employment', In : *Profile of the Child Labour in India*, Barnabas, A.P., *et al* (Eds), Ministry of Social Welfare, Government of India
12. Pattanaik, M., 1979, Child Labour in India: Size and Occupational Distribution, Chaturvedi. T.N. (Ed) *Administration for Child Welfare*, Indian Institute of Public Administration publication, p. 136.
13. Jain, S.N., 1979, *Child and the Law*, New Delhi.
14. *Report of the Committee on Child Labour* (Gurupada Swamy), Ministry of Labour, Government of India, 1979.
15. *Child Labour: A Threat to Health and Development*, Defence for Children, Geneva, 1981.
16. Juyal, B.N., 1985, *Child Labour and Exploitation in the Carpet Industry*, Indian Social Institute, New Delhi, pp. 33.
17. Dinesh, B.M., 1988, *Economic Activities of Children*, Daya Publishing House, Delhi.
18. Jha, A., 1989, The Problem of Child labour, *Third Concept*, March, pp. 29.
19. Tripathy, S.N., 1989, *Bonded Labour in India*, Discovery Publishing House, New Delhi.
20. Tripathy, S.N., 1997, *Migrant Child Labour in India*, Mohit Publications, New Delhi.
21. Fyfe, Alec, 1989, *Child Labour*, Polity Press Publications.
22. Benjamin, J., 1990, Child Labour: The Quest for Socio-Economic Inquiry, *Third Concept*, December, pp. 33-36.
23. Sharma, B.K., *et al*, 1990, *Child Labour and Urban Informal Sector*, Deep and Deep Publications, Delhi.
24. Weiner, M., 1991, *The Child and the State in India*, Oxford University Press.
25. Panicker, R. and Nangia, P., 1992, *Working and Street Children in Delhi*, National Labour Institute, Child labour Cell, Noida.
26. Pandey, R., 1993, *Street Children in Kanpur*, National Labour Institute, Child labour Cell, Noida.
27. Farooqui, V., 1993, Cruel Treatment and Abuse of Girl Child, In : Kapur, P. (Ed), *Girl Child and Family Violence*, Har Anand Publications, p. 199.
28. Varma, A.P. and Jain, M., 1995, *Trade Unions Child Labour and IPEC*, National Labour Institute, Child labour Cell, Noida.

29. Sahoo, U.C., 1995, *Child Labour in Agrarian Society*, Rawat Publications, New Delhi.
30. Anandharajakumar. P., 1997, Child Labour in India: Causes and Consequences, *Third Concept*, June, pp. 52-55.
31. Burra, Neera, 1997, *Child Labour in India*, Oxford University Press, Delhi.
32. Rao, R., 1998, Women Workers in Beedi Industry, *Social Welfare*, Volume 45, Number 5, August.
33. Jawa, R., 1999, "Female Child Labour and Poverty", In : *Need for New Strategy to Eradicate Poverty*, Gaur, K.D., (Ed), Manak Publication, New Delhi.
34. Kumar, B., 2000, *Problems of Working Children*, A.P.H. Publishing Corporation, New Delhi.
35. Khare, V., 2002, Human Rights in India: Issues and Perspective, A Case Study of Child labour, *Third Concept*, September, pp. 31-33.
36. Nanjunda, D.C., 2005, Panchayats and Rural Child Labour, *Third Concept*, September, pp. 37-40.

2
Anatomy of Child Labour

"Child shows the man as morning shows the day".

—John Milton

Children are the future of the society. The future of the nation becomes dim when they are compelled to languish in oppression. *Oxford Advanced Learner's Dictionary* defined child as "A young human who is not yet an adult". The child population of the country can be categorized as infants who are below 1 year, toddlers in the age group of 1 to 2 years, pre-schoolers in the age group of 3-5 year and the other in the age group of 6-14 year. While the children as a group requires special attention but for the present analysis we are more concerned about the children in the age bracket of 6-14 years. Very often these children are engaged in economic activities in the form of 'child labour'.

What is Child Labour?

Defining child labour is not as simple as it may appear because it encompasses three difficult words to define the concept "Child, work, and labour". Different authors have defined the child labour in a number of ways. Let us analyse the concept.

Encyclopaedia Boitannica defined the "child labour" as the employment of children under the age of physical maturity in jobs requiring long hours.[1]

Dr. S.N. Jain explains the "Child labour" as any activity done by children which either contributes to production, gives adult free time, facilitates the work of other or substitutes for the employment of others".[2]

Article 24 of the Indian Constitution prohibits employment of children below the age of 14 year in any factory or mine or hazardous occupation. Here "no child below 14 year means all those who fall under 14 years of age are considered as children and at the same time who are 14 year or more need not fall under non-children" (adolescent) category.

The Child Labour (Prohibition and Regulation) Act, 1986 defined the 'child' as a person who has not completed his / her fourteenth year of age.

Defining 'Child Labour' is not as simple as it may appear. Regarding the meaning of child labour there are basically three different schools of thought. One school of thought considers all out-of-school children as child labourers (Government of Andhra Pradesh, the Study Group of report on 'Women and Child Labour' for the Labour Commission corroborates this view) (Sinha 2000; Burra 1995). Another school of thought supports the conventional definition of 'child labour', where it should be distinguished from 'child work' (Lieten 2003). Yet another school of thought believes that the work, which affects education, growth and development of children, could be considered as 'child labour' (Mishra 2000).

Very often three terms viz., 'child work', 'child labour' and 'child exploitation' are used synonymously. However, a close look reveals that the former has got a positive sense whereas the other two terms have negative attributes. The phenomenon of child work is not new to modern society. Its origin can be traced back to human civilization. In the early phase of the evolution of the society, the process of learning by doing, child work was considered as a part of the process of socialization. Meanwhile, in the changing situation of society attitude towards children and the nature of work they are performing, undergoes a significant change. The nature of work, working conditions, employment relations were found to be unsuitable to children's growth and development. The school as an institution comes up as the best place for the all round development of the child. In the process, the norms have been changed and it is considered that no child should work and that all children must be in school.

All forms of work by children should not be considered deleterious. In fact, work as a direct fulfilment of child's natural abilities and creative potentialities is always conductive to his health, growth and development. Work by its very nature is enriching. The basic attributes of work are purpose, plan and freedom. When they are conspicuously absent, work becomes labour and will come in the way of the enfoldment of the child's natural abilities and creative potentialities (*Report of the Committee on Child Labour*). "The function of work in childhood should therefore be primarily developmental and not economic. Children's work as a social good, is the direct, antithesis of child labour as a social evil".

Work when taken-up as a means for the fulfilment of some other needs, becomes enslaving in character and deleterious in its impact. Labour is work of the latter type irrespective of the degree of strain or exploitation involved in it. Labour in case of the child, especially is harmful because the energy that should have been expended on the nurturing of his latent powers is consumed for the purpose of bare survival. Child Labour assumes the character of a social problem in as much as it hinders, arrests or distorts the natural growth processes and prevents the child from attaining his full-blown manhood.

What is 'child exploitation'? This is nothing but the use of 'child labour' in a pejorative sense. It conveys an impression of something obnoxious, hateful and carrying an element of exploitation (Nagaraj 1998). Labour becomes an absolute evil and danger when: child is required to work beyond his physical and mental capacity, labour involves extraction of excessive profits, nature of energy generated by a child is appropriated by some others and the child is left with a fraction of it, hours of employment interfere with his education, recreation and rest, wages do not commensurate with the quantum of work, the occupation engaged endangers his health and safety.

Work turns into exploitation when children: work too young, work too long hours, work for little pay, work under slave like arrangement and work in hazardous conditions. To put in nutshell, the important characteristics of child exploitation are: working too young, working long hours, working under physical, social or psychological strain.

The opinion of Claude Dumont chief of the ILO's conditions of work and welfare facilities branch, settles the debate of child work and child labour. In his word "Naturally, the ILO is not against all forms of child work, we have no problem with the little girl who helps her mother with the housework or cooking, or the boy or girl who does unpaid work in a small family business. Quite the contrary, by performing simple tasks or helping in a family enterprise, they can pick up skills that are handed down from generation to generation, and this makes it easier for the children to integrate into society. This sort of work can even be a source of satisfaction for the child because the child assumes its responsibilities and can be proud of what it can do. The same is true of those odd jobs that children may occasionally take on to earn a little pocket money to buy something they really want, provided of course, that the odd job is not dangerous or illegal."

In response to a query what exactly do you mean of the word child labour? Claude Dumont responded unequivocally that the ILO is opposed to work carried out by children, either as paid or independent labour, when this work has become a daily necessity which inevitably deprives the child at the educational and social level: when this work may harm the child's safety and health. The ILO also opposes all forms of work, which can offend children's morality. Hence, child labour is defined as work, which deprives the child of its 'right to childhood'.

However, in practice we consider all children who are involved in economic activity, which includes paid and unpaid work, work within the household and outside and self-employed, and refer to them as child labourers.

Why Child Labour?

Universally condemned as an intolerable disrespect for human dignity and an enormous waste of human resources child labour persists nonetheless. There is no single determining cause for the prevalence of child labour. It is a multi-dimensional one.

Child labour is the product of numerous factors, viz., poverty, unemployment, unequal distribution of assets, low health among

poor, migration to the cities due to industrialization and urbanization, the tradition of family occupation, low literacy rate, lack of education facility to all, dropouts, reluctant parent to send their children to school, the dismal picture of school, social acceptance of child labour, superstitious believe and lack of awareness of child rights, lack of proper implementation of the legislation, Ineffective administrative set-up , lack of political will, inadequate legislation for unorganized sector and above all cheap and trouble free, less assertive working group etc.

To have a better understanding let us club the above-mentioned factors into different sub-groups of the multidimensional picture as portrayed in Table 2.1.

Table 2.1

Causes of Child Labour

1. Economic factors:
   - Unequal & Iniquitous Distribution of Assets
   - Poverty
   - Low Per Capita Income
   - Low Standard of Living
   - High Indebtedness
   - Malnutrition & Low Health Care
   - Unemployment & Underemployment
   - Industrialisation & Urbanisation
2. Socio-Cultural Factors:
   - Defective Social System
     - (*i*) Illiteracy of Parents
     - (*ii*) The Process of Socialisation
     - (*iii*) Prestige for earning child
   - Unhealthy Cultural System
     - (*i*) Discriminating Treatment to Girl Child
     - (*ii*) Lack of Universalisation of Education
   - Obsolete Education System
     - (*i*) Non-Compulsory of Primary Education

Table 2.1 (Contd.)...

	(*ii*) Dismal Picture of the School
	(*iii*) Traditional & Poor Quality of Education
	(*iv*) Lack of adequate Resources
	(*v*) School out of Reach
3. Political & Administrative Factors:	
	• Less Spending by Govt. for Primary Education
	• Inadequate Social Welfare Programme
	• Sluggish Nature of the Administrative Machinery for working of Poverty Alleviation Programmes
4. Legal factors:	
	• Inadequacy of Labour Laws
	• Flaws inherited by the Existing Laws
	• Failure to Implement the Laws in Proper way
5. Employer Friendly Factors:	
	• Child labour is Cheap
	• Children are Docile in Character
	• Child Labourers are Unorganised in Nature

Economic Factors

Poverty is the root cause of many social evils. Child labour is one among these. It is rightly remarked, "**necessity knows no law**". So, how can a law prohibiting child labour be effective when it is a by-product of an economic necessity? Statistics shows that even after 60 years of independence 26 per cent of our total population is living below poverty line. Nearly one third of the metropolitan populations live in slums.

Poverty is by far the predominant reason for which children become child labourers. It forces children to work to meet subsistence household expenses, and to attenuate the risk of debts, bad harvests, illness or loss of work of the adult members. When the income of the family is insufficient to meet the needs of its members, parents are forced to send their children to work. Given a choice most parents would not like their children to work. The dilemma can appear straight forward: either have the child work or have the family face starvation. This pathetic condition forces the parents to accept their children to be employed.

Children in bonded labour often represent the continuation of age-old tradition of slavery. Poverty compels families to sell children into bonded labour in return for either a lump sum of money or debt repayment. Families living under debt bondage forbids the parents the opportunity of decision making power regarding their children's upbringing.

Poverty indicates lack of self-sufficiency in livelihood or economic instability of family. As a result Children work to supplement the income of their family. The employment of children in different units indicates helplessness and poverty of the family. To avoid economic crisis in the family children are bound to work in less remunerative work.

Some authors have observed that poverty is not the cause but often the consequence of child labour. Child labour perpetuates poverty on a large scale since a good number of children lacking in skills and education grow up as unskilled workers and follow the same benighted course in their future life.

Large family size is the outcome of poverty and illiteracy. The needs of the family are dependent on the size of the family. When the need goes up, there is bound to be an increase in expenditure. This leads to the burden of earning more by all the family members irrespective of age. Hence, children get engaged in work.

Socio-cultural Factors

Sociological factors, too, have their share of this scourge. The tradition of family occupation often motivates the child to become a breadwinner. In some cases the children themselves prefer to join the labour force because of the dignity, freedom and responsibility attached to him as a contributing member of the family. Analysis shows that very often children left school not due to poverty but on account of the acceptance of the traditional activity of the family.

One of the strong causes of child labour is deeply embedded in the Indian tradition of home based or family occupations. In a caste stratified society like India most occupations and crafts are family enterprises based on inherited skills and secrets. So, most of the children were expected to learn these skills and secrets from their fathers. In case of girl children, they share the responsibility of the mother in doing housework. Traditionally this was considered necessary and reinforced a fatalistic attitude that one was born to perform certain tasks. In this circumstance there was very little possibility of improving one's position in the society.

The educational system adds yet another dimension to the prevalence of the child labour problem. Education is one of the important aspects of social life. But unfortunately, the need of education is not realised by many of the parents. Parental attitudes often play a major role in sending child to work. On account of illiteracy many parents in India do not want to educate their children. They concentrate on the present needs of the family. They have developed a negative opinion towards education in a sense that education will give its benefit in future but present needs are more important than the future. Such notion creates unfavourable practice in the field of educational development.

In rural areas schooling facilities are scarce and inaccessible to certain segment of population. In many places, schools do not attract children and presents a drab and dismal picture. Likewise, lack of infrastructure facilities, congenial environment and motivation, parents do not take interest towards education of their children. Even though primary education is in principle 'free', parents often face indirect costs such as uniforms, textbooks, tutoring, and even unofficial payments to teachers. Impoverished parents who choose to send children to school instead of work incur not only these indirect costs, but lose the children's income as well. Under such circumstance they are bound to discourage their children from studying. These are the factors mainly associated with never enrolled children / dropouts but the following are 'push outs' for the enrollers. The retention rate of the pupils in the school (particularly in rural area) mostly depends on the skill of the teachers to make classes more interesting. They should avoid being mechanical in their routine and try to divert at frequent intervals. Playing games, telling moral stories, teaching vocational skills will automatically enhance the interest of children in school, but, the teachers very often lack theses skills.

Moreover, the mounting pressure of unemployment among educated youth undermines the faith of the rural poor in the efficacy and pay-off of education. Most of the children finding non-availability of school going facilities at initial stage and then seek some jobs as an alternative. The practice of child labour is not only existent among the non-school going children but by and large a sizeable number of boarders attend agriculture and they do not turn up in the hostels for days together. A study "Evaluation of Centrally-sponsored Schemes of Boys' Hostels for Scheduled Castes" conducted in Telangana region of Andhra Pradesh reveals that many boarders follow the same practice. Few of them work with private units on daily wages to meet their pocket and education expenditure.[3]

National Commission on Labour has observed that, child labour and non-schooling of children have a significant linkage among the poorer section of the society. Child labour is widespread on account of the reason that the primary education is not compulsory. Children who are out of schools perform odd duties for long hours under subhuman conditions at wages below normal. Parents of most of these children are poor and deprived of education. Unless children are able to go to school, it will not be possible for them to break out of the illiteracy trap. Hence, it is highly essential that the primary education should be compulsory to have a dent over the problem of child labour.

There is an ongoing debate whether compulsory education will act as a panacea for child labour problem. This point has also been raised in the ministry of Home Affairs Memorandum of Action on the Report of the National Human Rights Commission (NHRC). A study in Kerela shows that on account of near-universal primary education the incidence of child labour is very low. The study further notes that school attendance protects children from dangerous labour practices and sets limits on what type of work a child can perform. Study also pointed out that in Kerela the incidence of child labour is very low. This trend is not due to strict enforcement of child labour legislation but due to development of a healthy culture of child education and it is this culture that mostly keeps children out of labour market. Hence, it is necessary to build up this kind of culture and awareness throughout the country by sensitizing and mobilizing the civil society as well as people's representatives.

Political and Administrative Factors

Children have neither voice nor any political constituency. Children have no voting right to elect the representatives of the Government, so their problems are not properly presented in the parliament. There is lack of political will among legislators to put forth the problem of child labour and other related issues in a proper manner as there is no pressure in this regard. These children are mere spectators to the priorities and programmes proposed for them. They can neither express their view nor can demand.

As Myron Winer pointed out that the Indian Government spends less on primary education than most other Asian countries and "puts a disproportionate share of its educational resources on higher education, a political decision which has benefited the middle classes, while leaving the rural and urban poor educationally impoverished".[4]

The National Human Rights Commission (NHRC) in its Annual Report (1995-96) has expressed the unequivocal view that the problem of child labour will persist until the free compulsory education for all up to the age of 14 years is realized. In a letter addressed to the presidents of all major political parties in India, the chairman of NHRC observed that, despite the provision of Art 45 of the Indian constitution the number of illiterates are still high. For making primary education compulsory, there is need for strong political will and, if necessary, redeployments of national resources. However, recently Government of India and several state governments are taking a number of steps under the programme of Sarva Siksha Abhiyana (Education for All) for popularization / Universalization of primary education. Mid-day meal, books at free of cost, school dress to girl child at free of cost, play-way method for teaching, and beautification of the school campus are some of the steps taken by the government for mobilizing the parents and children towards education and educational environment. Central Government in its budget (2004-05) introduced an educational cess for funding exclusively the primary education. These are some of the welcome steps undertaken by the Government.[5]

The social assistance programmes such as family benefit, old age pension etc. are in the pre-stage. The allowances of such programmers are so meager that it could hardly make survive a needy family. For example in old age pension Rs. 100 per month or under family benefit scheme (Rs. 5,000 in case natural death or Rs.10,000 in accidental death of the primary bread winner) are not sufficient. As a result, a needy family cannot stop their children to work because they have to fulfil the basic needs of the family.

The rural development programmes are also not functioning properly to ameliorate the conditions of the rural poor. Lack of proper implementation of the poverty eradication programmes is mainly responsible for this. Administrative machinery should be geared up for the successful working of these poverty alleviation programmes. So that the have-nots are able to improve their economic standard and no more dependent on their children's contribution to the income of the family.

Legal Factors

Inadequacy of labour legislation to protect child labour, lacuna in existing laws and failure to implement the laws are three important reasons why more and more children are drifted into the labour force.

Regarding the first situation, the labour legislation has yet to cover the most important avenues of employment in the country. No legislation was ever passed to protect child labour in agriculture, domestic services, small-scale industries and other unorganized and informal sectors. Surprisingly the Amendment in 1986 has deliberately legalized the child labour in plantation industry, may be with a view to bring it down in par with agricultural sector, instead of bringing up the latter sector in par with the former. This is, in fact, regressive uniformly.

The lapses of enforcement machinery have indirectly inducted a major chunk of children into the labour market. A dark patch in the whole act is that it empowers only factory inspectors to lodge complaints of such violations. While inadequacy of man and material for inspection and supervision on the one hand and the callousness or the indifferent attitude of the inspecting authorities on the other hand are mainly responsible for the violation of labour laws by the employers. The penalties for such violations in themselves are not stringent enough and social activists, voluntary organizations and concerned citizens are not allowed to function as watch dogs. In this circumstance there is ample scope for corruption and perpetuation of such nefarious practices. What is even more surprising is that the trade unions which have been fighting for better wages and working conditions, have shown little interest in this problem. These suffering children do not happen to be their vote banks. Thus, ineffective implementation of labor laws calls for more teeth to the existing administrative and organization arrangements.

Further almost all labour legislations prohibiting child labour concentrates on hazardous occupations. No doubt 'hazardous occupations' are in fact dangerous to the child worker, but in a sense, every occupation is hazardous, for it not only retards the child's growth and development rather hampers growth and development of the nation. Economic growth is impeded because poorly educated children in this generation will mean fewer qualified and skilled adults enter the labour force in the next generation

Employer Friendly Factors

Child labour is widespread all over the world because of the reasons that employers find it inexpensive and extremely profitable. Though children are less productive than adults, they are easier to abuse, less assertive, and less able to claim their rights and can be made to work longer hours with little food, poor accommodation, and no benefits. Children are paid a fraction of what an adult will be paid for the same job. Children work for long hours with small wages and are more docile and easier to manage than adults. Child labour is trouble-free, since children cannot organize agitations by themselves and being minors, the membership of the trade unions is not thrown open to them. Neither they can demand any overtime, nor the medical and similar facilities. They are more submissive and obedient to the employer. Hence, the employers prefer children to work.

In a study undertaken by Susan Crawford in carpet-weaving workshop of Pakistan finds that the majority of owners admitted that availability of cheap child labor in the area was the main reason for selection of a particular area to start their business. They hire children because they work for longer hours with lower remuneration. However, they feel that they are indeed doing a good job to these children, who would not anyway get any opportunity for education by providing money, which their families need.

All of the above factors, alone or in combination, contribute to the proliferation of child labour. Research is needed to show which predominates in any particular situation. Poverty undoubtedly an important cause, but evidence from field study shows that a significant proportion of child labour comes from households above poverty line, and especially among girls. This appears to be the result of low educational returns.

Extent of Child Labour

In this section an attempt has been made to explore the magnitude of the problem of child labour. Estimating the extent of child labour is not an easy task. Moreover, the magnitude and structure of child labour system is vast and varied.

International Level

International Labour Organisation (ILO) estimates some 250 million children between the ages of 5 and 14 are working in developing countries, of this total around 120 million are fulltime worker and rest are part-time workers.[6] Some 61 per cent of child workers are found in Asia, 32 per cent in Africa and 0.7 per cent in Latin America (Table 2.2).

Table 2.2. Percentage of Economically Active Children (5-14 years of age, 1995)

Continent	*Percent of Child Labour*	*Numbers in Million*
Asia	61	153
Africa	32	80
Latin America	0.7	17.5
Other	6.3	

Combining various official documents ILO estimates that more than 73 million children in the age group of 10-14 were economically active in 1995. This represents 13.2 per cent of all 10-14 year olds around the world. The greatest numbers were found in Asia - 44.6 million (13 per cent) followed by Africa and Latin America, 23.6 million (26.3 per cent) and 5.1 million (9.8 per cent) respectively.

"But this is only part of the picture", says Assafa Bequele, child labour specialist of ILO. "No reliable figures on workers under 10 are available though their numbers, we know, are significant. The same is true of children between 14 and 15 on whom few reports exist. If all of these could be counted and if proper account were taken of the domestic work performed full-time by girls, the total number of child workers around the world today might well be in the hundreds of millions".

While child labour is found in all regions of the world, it is overwhelmingly a developing country phenomenon. In absolute terms, it is Asia, as the most densely populated region of the world that has most child workers. But in relative terms Africa comes first. In per centage terms Africa has 41 per cent of all children between the ages of 5 and 14 involved in economic activity, in Asia it is 21 per cent and in Latin America it is 17 per cent. The majority of children are employed in agriculture either on the family farm or on a commercial exploitation.[7]

The proportion of working children has been much higher in rural than in urban areas - nine out of ten are engaged in agriculture or related activities. In urban area child labour has increased on account of urbanization and industrialization. ILO observed that working children are found mainly in trade and services (especially in domestic help) and to a lesser extent in the manufacturing sector.

The vast majority of child workers are employed in small production units of the urban informal sector and the rural traditional sector. The modern sector plays a relatively minor role in absorbing child labour, with exception of plantation in some countries. However, medium-sized and large enterprises may contribute indirectly to the employment of child labour through their practice of contracting out part of their production to small informal workshops or home workers who make intensive use of child labour.

Statistical survey conducted by ILO has shown that the economic activity of 75 per cent of children between the ages of 5 to 14 takes place in a family enterprise setting. The child labour force consists mainly of unpaid family workers. Although it is a common practice everywhere, child labour in family enterprises is more prevalent in rural than in urban areas. Child wage-earners are to be found more often in urban area than rural areas. The older the children, the more likely they are to be in this category.

Statistics suggest that more boys than girls work. Among developing regions, Africa has the highest participation rate of girls, i.e., approximately 37 per cent, as against this in Asia it is 20 per cent and in Latin America 11 per cent girls work as child labour. But it should be borne in mind that the number of working girls is often underestimated by statistical survey as they usually do not take into account full-time housework performed by many girl children.[8]

At the international level, attention focuses mainly on children employed in Third World countries and predominantly export industries, such as, textiles, clothing, carpets and footwear. Moreover, in the export sectors, child labour appears to be more common in plantation than in manufacturing.

Economically active children in selected countries are shown in Table 2.3. In Asian countries Bhutan is having highest child labour, i.e., 55 per cent followed by Nepal with 45 per cent. Among African countries Mali tops the rank with 55 per cent followed by Burkina Faso 51 per cent. Haiti in Latin American countries constitutes highest per centage of child labour, i.e., 25 per cent followed by Guatemala with 16 per cent.

Table 2.3. Economically Active Children in Selected Countries (10-14 years of age, 1995)

Continent	*Country*	*Percentage of Child Labour*
Asia	Bhutan	55
	Nepal	45
	Bangladesh	30
	India	14
Africa	Mali	54
	Burkina Faso	51
	Burundi	48
Latin America	Haiti	25
	Brazil	16
	Guatemala	16

Source: *Economic activities population. Estimates and Projections 1950-2010*, 4th edition on published data available from ILO Bureau of Statistics, ILO Geneva.

Child labour in India

Population Census, conducted once in every ten years and the quinquennial sample surveys of National Sample Survey Organisation (NSSO) on employment and unemployment are two main sources of data on overall employment and unemployment in the country. These two sources also provide workforce data by age distribution. From this one can obtain information on the incidence of child labour. The employment data from NSSO is more reliable than census as the former has well trained investigators. However, if one wants data at the district level, we have to rely on Census only.

Estimates based on Census data show that the magnitude of child labour has increased from 13.3 million in 1951 to 13.6 million in 1981 but declined to a level of 12.6 million in 2001. The 55th Round of the National Sample Survey, carried out by the NSSO in 1999-2000, indicates that there are about 10.4 million working children (Table 2.4).

Table 2.4. Extent of Child Labour (5-14 years) in India (figures in million).

Census	*1951*	*1961*	*1971*	*1981*	*1991*	*2001*
Child Labour	13.3	14.4	10.7	13.6	11.2	12.6
NSSO Rounds	1983	1985	1987	1990	93-94	99-2000
Child Labour	17.4	17.6	13.0	18.2	13.2	10.4

Source: Child Labour Facts and Figures: An Analysis of Census 2001, ILO, 2007

As compared to 1991 Census, there has been an increase of 10.68 per cent in workers aged 5-14 years in 2001 Census (excluding the State of J&K). Between 2001 census and 1991 census, in terms of absolute number, the category of main workers aged 5-14 years has decreased considerably by well over one-third (36.97 per cent). However, over the same period there has been a manifold increase of marginal workers aged 5-14 years (207.10 per cent). This is clear from the Table 2.5 which presents data on absolute number of child labour in 1991 and 2001 census.

Table 2.5. Distribution of Child Labour (5-14 year) by their work status

Census Year	*Main Workers*	*Marginal Workers*	*Total Workers*
1991	9082141	2203208	11285349
2001	5778991	6887386	12666377

Source: Child Labour Facts and Figures: An Analysis of Census 2001, ILO, 2007

Table 2.6. Child Labour by Work Status and Sex, 2001 Census

Category	*Main Workers*	*Marginal Workers*	*Total Workers*	*Non Workers*
Male	3596904	3207432	6804336	114933897
Female	2182087	3679954	5862041	125563374
Total	5778991	6887386	12666377	240497271

Source: Child Labour Facts and Figures: An Analysis of Census 2001, ILO, 2007

Table 2.6 depicts the distribution of child population in the age group of 5-14 years by work status and sex as per the Census 2001. Data show that a major part of main workers are boys, whereas girls constitute mainly marginal workers.

Table 2.7 shows the distribution of child workers according to sex and nativity. As estimated in 1991 census total 11.28 million child labour in the country 54.86 per cent are male and 45.14 per cent are females. Regarding rural-urban distribution of child labour, the data explains that 90.86 per cent of child workers are found in rural areas and remaining 9.14 per cent in urban areas. 2.20 million workers are termed as marginal workers and the rest 9.08 million child workers are main workers. In per centag. basis the former is 19.5 per cent and the later is 80.5 per cent.

Table 2.7. Percentage Distribution of Child Workers by Sex and Nativity

		Main Worker	*Marginal Worker*	*Total*
Rural area	Male	4,960,391	496,660	5,457,051(48.36)
	Female	3,166,815	1,629,334	4,796,149(42.50)
	Total	8,127,206	2,125,994	10,253,200(90.86)
Urban Area	Male	702,835	29,948	732,783(6.5)
	Female	252,100	47,266	299,366(2.64)
	Total	954,935	77,214	1,032,149(9.14)
	Grand Total	9,082,141	2,203,208	11,285349(100)
	Rural:	90.86%,	Male:	54.86%
	Urban:	9.14%,	Female:	45.14%

Note: Figures in parentheses represents per centage.
Source: India, Ministry of labour (2000), New Delhi.

According to 2001 Census of India the total work force in the age group of 5-14 years is 126.67 lakhs. Out of this 57.80 lakhs (45.6 per cent) are main workers and 68.87 lakhs (54.4 per cent) are marginal workers. The share of workers in the country aged 5-14 years in the total population of the concerned age group turns out to be 5.00 per cent. However, the share of workers aged 5-14 years in the total work force of the country is 3.15 per cent.

In 1981, the total work force in the country was about 223 million of which working children were 13.6 million, which worked out to be about 6 per cent of the total work force. In 1991, the working population of India was 314 million and child workers were 11.28 million, which constituted 3.59 per cent of the total workforce. However, in 2001 India has a total workforce of 402 million and child workers are 12.6 million, which constitutes 3.15 per cent of total work force. This is illustrated in Table 2.8.

Table 2.8. Percentage of Child labour to Total Work Force in Different Census

Census	*Work Force*	*Child Labour*	*% of Child Labour to Work Force*
1981	223	13.56	6.00
1991	314	11.28	3.59
2001	402	12.66	3.15

Source: Census of India, 1981, 1991, 2001, Government of India.

There are significant regional disparities in the incidence of child labour. Table 2.9 provides the extent of child labour in different states. Table 2.10 represents the per centage of child labour across States from various Censuses. It is interesting to note that a poorer state like Orissa has lower incidence of child labour as compared to Southern States like Andhra Pradesh and Karnataka. Data show that the highest number of child labour is found in Andhra Pradesh. The other States that follow Andhra Pradesh are Uttar Pradesh, Madhya Pradesh, Maharashtra, Karnataka, Bihar, Rajasthan, West Bengal and Tamil Nadu. These nine States together constitute around 85 per cent of the total child labour. In the contrary the States Punjab, Haryana, Himachal Pradesh, Kerala, Meghalaya, Manipur, Tripura, Nagaland, and Sikkim share less than four per cent of total child workers in India. About two-thirds of total child labour in India is concentrated in six states, namely Andhra

Pradesh, Uttar Pradesh, Madhya Pradesh, Maharashtra, Karnataka and Bihar (Table 2.110). Table 2.11 depicts the concentration of child labour in six states in the order of ranking.

Table 2.9. Statewise Distribution of Working Children (5-14 years) in Various Censuses

Sl. No.	*Name of the State/UT*	*1971*	*1981*	*1991*	*2001*[1]
1.	Andhra Pradesh	1627492	1951312	1661940	1363339
2.	Assam*	239349	**	327598	351416
3.	Bihar	1059359	1101764	942245	1117500
4.	Gujarat	518061	616913	523585	485530
5.	Haryana	137826	194189	109691	253491
6.	Himachal Pradesh	71384	99624	56438	107774
7.	Jammu & Kashmir	70489	258437	**	175630
8.	Karnataka	808719	1131530	976247	822615
9.	Kerela	111801	92854	34800	26156
10.	Madhya Pradesh	1112319	1698597	1352563	1065259
11.	Maharashtra	988357	1557756	1068427	764075
12.	Chhattisgarh				364572
13.	Manipur	16380	20217	16493	28836
14.	Meghalaya	30440	44916	34633	53940
15.	Jharkhanda				407200
16.	Uttaranchal				70183
17.	Nagaland	13726	16235	16467	45874
18.	Orissa	492477	702293	452394	377594
19.	Punjab	232774	216939	142868	177268
20.	Rajasthan	587389	819605	774199	1262570
21.	Sikkim	15661	8561	5598	16457
22.	Tamil Nadu	713305	975055	578889	418801
23.	Tripura	17490	24204	16478	21756
24.	Uttar Pradesh	1326726	1434675	1410086	1927997
25.	West Bengal	511443	605263	711691	857087

Sl. No.	*Name of the State/UT*	*1971*	*1981*	*1991*	*2001*****
26.	Andaman & Nicober Islands	572	1309	1265	1960
27.	Arunchal Pradesh	17925	17950	12395	18482
28.	Chandigarh	1086	1986	1870	3779
29.	Dadra & Nagar Haveli	3102	3615	4416	4274
30	Delhi	17120	25717	27351	41899
31	Daman & Diu	7391	9378	941	729
32	Goa			4656	4138
33	Lakshdweep	97	56	34	27
34	Mizoram***		6314	16411	26265
35	Pondichery	3725	3606	2680	1904
	Total	10753985	13640870	11285349	12666377

Source: Downloaded from Internet.

Note: * 1971 Census figures of Assam include figures of Mizoram.

** Census couldn't be conducted.

*** Census figures 1971 in respect of Mizoram included under Assam.

**** Includes marginal workers also.

Table 2.10. Percentage Distribution of Working Children (5-14 years) in Various Censuses

Sl. No.	*Name of the State / UT*	*1971*	*1981*	*1991*	*2001*
1.	Andhra Pradesh	15.13	14.30	14.73	10.76
2.	Assam*	2.23	0.00	2.90	2.77
3.	Bihar	9.85	8.08	8.35	8.82
4.	Gujarat	4.82	4.52	4.64	3.83
5.	Haryana	1.28	1.42	0.97	2.00
6.	Himachal Pradesh	0.66	0.73	0.50	0.85
7.	Jammu & Kashmir	0.66	1.89	0.00	1.39
8.	Karnataka	7.52	8.30	8.65	6.49
9.	Kerela	1.04	0.68	0.31	0.21

Sl. No.	*Name of the State / UT*	*1971*	*1981*	*1991*	*2001*
10.	Madhya Pradesh	10.34	12.45	11.99	8.41
11.	Maharashtra	9.19	11.42	9.47	6.03
12.	Chhattisgarh	0.00	0.00	0.00	2.88
13.	Manipur	0.15	0.15	0.15	0.23
14.	Meghalaya	0.28	0.33	0.31	0.43
15.	Jharkhanda	0.00	0.00	0.00	3.21
16.	Uttaranchal	0.00	0.00	0.00	0.55
17.	Nagaland	0.13	0.12	0.15	0.36
18.	Orissa	4.58	5.15	4.01	2.98
19.	Punjab	2.16	1.59	1.27	1.40
20.	Rajasthan	5.46	6.01	6.86	9.97
21.	Sikkim	0.15	0.06	0.05	0.13
22.	Tamil Nadu	6.63	7.15	5.13	3.31
23.	Tripura	0.16	0.18	0.15	0.17
24.	Uttar Pradesh	12.34	10.52	12.49	15.22
25.	West Bengal	4.76	4.44	6.31	6.77
26.	Andaman & Nicober Islands	0.01	0.01	0.01	0.02
27.	Arunchal Pradesh	0.17	0.13	0.11	0.15
28.	Chandigarh	0.01	0.01	0.02	0.03
29.	Dadra & Nagar Haveli	0.03	0.03	0.04	0.03
30.	Delhi	0.16	0.19	0.24	0.33
31.	Daman & Diu	0.07	0.07	0.01	0.01
32.	Goa	0.00	0.00	0.04	0.03
33.	Lakshdweep	0.00	0.00	0.00	0.00
34.	Mizoram ***	0.00	0.05	0.15	0.21
35.	Pondichery	0.03	0.03	0.02	0.02
	Total	100	100	100	100

Source: Same as Table 7

Table 2.11. Concentration of Child Labour in Six States

Sl.No.	*Name of the State*	*1971*	*1981*	*1991*	*2001*
1.	Andhra Pradesh	15.13	14.30	14.73	10.76
2.	Uttar Pradesh	12.34	10.52	12.49	15.22
3.	Madhya Pradesh	10.34	12.45	11.99	8.41
4.	Bihar	9.85	8.08	8.35	8.82
5.	Maharashtra	9.19	11.42	9.47	6.03
6.	Karnataka	7.52	8.30	8.65	6.49
7.	All other States	35.63	34.93	34.33	44.26
	Total	100	100	100	100

Source: Same as Table 8.

Child Labour in Orissa

As per the 2001 Census total children in the age group of 5-14 years in the state is 86.34 lakhs. Out of this 44.12 lakhs are boys and 42.44 lakhs are girls. Out of the total population, aged 5-14 years, 3.77 lakhs are workers and 82.57 lakhs are non-workers. Amongst the total work force, 1.10 lakhs (29.07 per cent) are main workers and 2.67 lakhs (70.93 per cent) are marginal workers. The share of workers, aged 5-14 years in the total work force of the state works out to be 2.64 per cent.

If we compare the child worker in Orissa in various Census, the estimated figure increases from 4.92 lakhs in 1971 to 7.02 lakhs in 1980, but declines steadily to 4.52 lakhs in 1991 and further to a low of 3.77 lakhs in recently concluded census of 2001 (Table 2.12).

Table 2.12. Extent of Child Labour (5-14 years) in Orissa (figures in lakhs)

Census	*1971*	*1981*	*1991*	*2001*
Child Labour	4.92	7.02	4.52	3.77

Source: Child Labour Facts and Figures: An Analysis of Census 2001, ILO, 2007

Table 2.13 depicts the distribution of child population in the age group of 5-14 years in Orissa by work status and sex as per the Census 2001. Data show that a major part of main workers are boys, whereas girls constitute mainly marginal workers.

Table 2.13. Child Labour by Work Status and Sex, 2001 Census

Category	*Main Workers*	*Marginal Workers*	*Total Workers*	*Non Workers*
Male	69401	113869	183270	4228725
Female	40359	153965	194324	4027896
Total	109760	267834	377594	8634215

Source: Child Labour Facts and Figures: An Analysis of Census 2001, ILO, 2007

As compared to 1991 Census, there has been a decrease of 16.53 per cent in workers aged 5-14 years in 2001 Census. Between 2001 and 1991 in terms of absolute number, the category of main workers aged 5-14 years has decreased considerably, i.e., 611.31 per cent. However, over the same period there has been a manifold increase of marginal workers aged 5-14 years (110.65 per cent). This is clear from Table 2.14 which presents data on absolute number of child labour in 1991 and 2001 census.

Table 2.14. Distribution of Child Labour (5-14 year) by their work status

Census Year	*Main Workers*	*Marginal Workers*	*Total Workers*
1991	325250	127144	452394
2001	109760	267834	377594

Source: Child Labour Facts and Figures: An Analysis of Census 2001, ILO, 2007

Table 2.15 gives the highlights of the results of child labour survey 1997, Orissa. The table shows that Navarangpur district tops the rank in the field of child labour. 15.19 per cent of total child labour of orissa is concentrated in the district of Navarangpur. This is followed by kalahandi (6.83 per cent), Koraput (6.30per cent), Rayagada (5.69 per cent), Bolangir (5.70 per cent), and Balasore (5.58 per cent). In six districts viz., Dhenkanal, Ganjam, Jagatsignpur, Khurda, Puri and Sundargarh the incidence of child labour is less than one per cent. Child worker is lowest in Jagatsinghpur district (0.2 per cent).

Out of 2,15,222 child labours in Orissa 23,761 (i.e., 11.04 per cent) are working in hazardous occupations and 1,91,461 (i.e., 88.96 per cent) children are engaged in Non-hazardous activities. Again among the non-hazardous job maximum numbers of child labourers are found in agriculture.

Table 2.15. Distribution of Child Labour in Hazardous and Non-Hazardous Activities

Sl. No.	*Name of the District*	*Hazardous*	*Non-Hazardous*	*Total*
1.	Angul	2775	252	3027
2.	Balasore	437	11582	12019(5.58)
3.	Bargarh	109	1979	2088
4.	Bhadrak	10	5387	5397
5.	Bolangir	1704	10571	12275(5.70)
6.	Boudh	29	6371	6400
7.	Cuttack	1531	5896	7424
8.	Deogarh	428	4482	4910
9.	Dhenkanal	33	1869	1902
10.	Gajapati	2028	8197	10225(4.75)
11.	Ganjam	860	1012	1872
12.	Jagatsingpur	8	404	412
13.	Jajpur	37	2020	2057
14.	Jharsuguda	1815	4869	6684
15.	Kalahandi	0	14710	14710(6.83)
16.	Kandhamal	0	6456	6456
17.	Keonjhar	113	4067	4180
18.	Kendrapara	177	6062	6239
19.	Khurda	69	1797	1866
20.	Koraput	234	13324	13558(6.30)
21.	Malkangir	2073	8217	10290
22.	Mayrbhanja	1074	20681	21755

Sl. No.	*Name of the District*	*Hazardous*	*Non-Hazardous*	*Total*
23.	Nabarangapur	1167	31517	32684(15.19)
24.	Nayaghara	137	2109	2246
25.	Nuapada	997	1220	2217
26.	Puri	25	912	937
27.	Rayagada	02	12240	12242(5.69)
28.	Sambalpur	4811	828	5639
29.	Sonepur	1015	1622	2637
30.	Sundargarh	63	808	871
	Total	23761 (11.04)	191461 (88.96)	215222 (100)

Source: Labour Statistics in Orissa, (2004) Government of Orissa, Bhubaneswar, pp 25.

Note: Figures in parentheses represents per centage.

The non-hazardous occupation includes agriculture, metals, bakery and biscuit making, cattle grazing, ice cream, agarbati rolling gardening, carpentry, doll making, news paper hawking, vendor and others such as shop and establishments, cycle repairing, tailoring, laundry, etc.

Table 2.16 represents the district wise distribution of child labour with respect to sex. As per 1997 survey except Angul, Keonjhar, Sambalpur, Deogarh and Jharsuguda in all other districts number of male child labour outnumber female child labour. In Orissa male child labour constitutes 56.47 per cent and female child labour is 43.53 per cent.

The districtwise information about the extent of child labour in 2001 Census is represented in Table 2.17. The latest information shows that child labour is concentrated in the district of Ganjam (10.3 per cent), followed by Mayurbhanja (8.73 per cent). Child labour is lowest in Jagatsinghapur district (0.64 per cent).

Table 2.16. District-wise distribution of male-female division of child workers in Orissa (in %)

Name of the District	*1971*		*1997*	
	Male	*Female*	*Male*	*Female*
Orissa	85.97	14.03	56.47	43.63
Balsore	91.72	8.78	54.47	45.53
Bhadrak			62.48	37.52
Bolangir	92.46	7.36	60.08	39.92
Sonepur			72.58	27.42
Cuttack	81.95	8.05	60.56	39.44
Kendrapara			67.41	32.59
Jagatsinghpur			68.93	31.07
Jajpur			76.42	23.58
Dhenkanal	91.94	8.06	63.46	36.54
Angul			38.62	61.38
Ganjam	77.80	22.20	53.21	46.79
Gajapati			51.20	48.80
Kalahandi	91.63	8.37	58.55	41.45
Nuapoda			83.13	16.87
Keonjhar	86.76	13.22	44.00	56.00
Koraput	85.56	14.44	52.50	47.50
Navarangnpur			56.90	43.10
Rayagada			60.91	39.09
Malkangiri			61.32	38.68
Mayurabhanja	76.55	23.45	53.66	46.34
Puri	91.10	8.90	79.51	20.49
Khurda			67.31	32.69
Nayagarh			78.54	21.46
Phulbani	78.70	22.30	52.30	47.70
Boudh			56.42	43.58
Sambalpur	83.37	16.63	30.77	69.23
Bargarh			67.43	32.57
Deogarh			47.74	52.26
Sundargarh	84.64	15.36	74.63	25.37
Jharsugada			42.04	57.96

Source: 1. *Atlas of the Child in India*, Moonis Raza, Suresh Nangia, Concept Publication Company (1986)

Table 2.17. Child Labour by Work Status at District Level in Orissa, 2001 Census

District	*Main Worker*	*Marginal Worker*	*Total Worker*
Angul	3276	7121	10397
Balangir	4646	10596	15242
Baleshwar	3510	6180	9690
Bargarh	3551	8305	13059
Baudh	1187	2792	3979
Bhadrak	2253	3143	5396
Cuttack	4025	7332	11357
Debagarh	585	2539	3124
Dhenkanal	1917	3362	5279
Gajapati	6730	16912	23642
Ganjam	12568	26379	38947
Jagatsinghapur	1159	1289	2448
Jajapur	1430	1812	3242
Jharsuguda	1137	1774	2911
Kalahandi	6523	16958	23481
Kandhamal	2219	9684	11903
Kendrapara	993	5278	6271
Kendujhar	3046	9695	12741
Khordha	4078	2496	6574
Koraput	6472	17538	24010
Malkangiri	3607	9920	13527
Mayurbhanj	8273	24721	32994
Nabarangapur	6248	23517	29765
Nayagarh	1707	3206	4913
Nuapada	1467	6575	8042
Puri	1691	1390	3081
Rayagada	5029	11953	16982
Samabalpur	4144	7224	11368
Sonapur	1365	3660	5025
Sundargarh	4924	14483	19407
Orissa (Total)	109760	267834	377594

Source: Child Labour Facts and Figures: An Analysis of Census 2001, ILO, 2007

Table 2.18. Number of Child Labour Detected in last five Years

District	*2000-01*	*2001-02*	*2002-03*	*2003-04*	*2004-05*	*Total*
Angul			Survey is under progress			
Balasore	-	-	-	-	17537	17537
Bargarh	-	993	-	114	-	1107
Bhadrak	-	-	-	5846	-	5846
Bolangir	-	-	25264	-	-	25264
Boudh	-	-	-	-	11306	11306
Cuttack	4210	-	-	7272	-	11482
Deogarh	-	-	-	-	9878	9878
Dhenkanal	-	-	-	10880	-	10880
Gajapati	802	2033	629	805	10628	14897
Ganjam	-	2555	2669	2633	2542	10399
Jagatsingpur	-	-	-	2901	-	2901
Jajpur	-	-	-	7758	-	7758
Jharsuguda	-	2760	1107	983	2207	7057
Kalahandi	369	927	1016	645	1194	4151
Kandhamal	-	-	-	-	14085	14085
Keonjhar	-	-	-	8710	-	8710

District	2000-01	2001-02	2002-03	2003-04	2004-05	Total
Kendrapara	-	-	-	-	8693	8693
Khurda	-	-	-	5800	-	5800
Koraput	-	2244	2693	-	-	4937
Malkangir			Survey is under progress			
Mayrbhanja			Survey is under progress			
Nabarangapur	-	-	17556	-	-	17556
Nayaghara	-	-	-	7345	-	7345
Nuapada	-	-	-	-	2834	2834
Puri	-	-	-	-	6185	6185
Rayagada	3697	3662	7930	5930	5930	27149
Sambalpur	1600	150	1850	2550	600	6750
Sonepur	-	-	-	-	12298	12298
Sundargarh	-	-	-	6445	-	6445
Total	10678	15324	60714	76617	105917	269250

Recently district-wise survey for identification of child labour has been conducted by the National Child Labour Project Societies and the State Labour Institute, which has been completed in respect of 27 districts. The result of the survey is given in Table 2.18.

Consequence of Child Labour

The State of the World's Children, 1997 states that child labour is a betrayal of child's right as a human being and an offence against civilization. Some activities associated with child labour are health hazardous in nature and some others are harmful because of lack of proper facilities, unhygienic atmosphere, dirtiness, overworking, and non-congenial environment.

Child labour is a social evil under which children are forced to do labour in tender age. Their delicate organs are bound to join labour force in odd circumstance for less payment. The industrial environment is harmful for their physical, mental, psychological and moral growth. They put in pressure to work in different unfavourable and non-congenial posture, darkness, dirtiness, improper ventilation and lighting. The polluted and harmful environment leads to various temporary and / or chronic deformities, disabilities of spinal, stunted growth, infectious disease and respiratory problems, children may be crippled physically / mentally by being forced to work too early in life.[9]

Many studies have pointed out that the prevalence of child labour caused a lot of debilitating impact on the mental, physical and psychological development of the children concerned.

A large scale ILO Survey in the Philippines found that more than 60 per cent of working children were exposed to chemical and biological hazards and that 40 per cent experienced serious injuries or illnesses.

Work at a low age is detrimental to healthy growth of the child. A comparative study carried out over a period of 17 years in India on both the children who attend school and the children who instead work in agriculture, industry or the service sector shows that working children grow up shorter and weigh less than school children (ILO, 1996).

In studies carried out in Mumbai, the health of children working in hotels, restaurant construction and elsewhere was found to be considerably inferior to that of a control group of non-working school children.

Neera Burra's (1987) study revealed that the sign of pneumoconiosis, tuberculosis and bronchitis are visible among the children working for a period of 5-6 years in the lock industry of Aligarh. According to the textbook of preventive and social medicine, pneumoconiosis is caused by dust particles with the size of 0.3 to 0.5 microns. If any body exposed to these dust particles for a longer period it may cause to fibrosis in the lungs, which may cripple a man and create a number of health complicacy in future life.

Beedi, lock, glass, slate, match, fireworks industry and power loom industries are the examples of intrinsically pernicious industries. Industries like gem polishing, diamond cutting and zari embroidery though not hazardous in nature but the working posture of the workers and the environment it self is not conducive. Hence, leads to physical deformity and mental strain.

Work at a low age is detrimental to healthy growth of the child. Working children exhibited symptoms of constant muscular, chest and abdominal pain, headaches, dizziness, respiratory infection, diarrhea and worm infection. On the other side, they quickly develop bad habits and barred immoral activities like cigarette smoking, chewing of pan masala, gambling, drinking of liquor, theft and robbery, etc.

Child worker accounts for a considerable share of migrant labour. While some children migrate along with their family members, others migrate alone. In both the cases child workers face a lot of trouble. They may become extremely isolated from their family member and community, consequently they may be affected by deficiency in health and nutrition apart from emotional deprivation. Being cut off from source of protection they are also exposed to abuse.

The most shocking part of the story is that the child sent to labour market and employed in hazardous occupations may become a dependant on the family for the rest of his life instead of contributing to the welfare of the family. Being deprived of the opportunities for proper physical, mental and moral development they repeat the cycle of their parent's misery. Strenuous work in a tender age has direct consequence on the child's development, both physical and mental. Therefore, occupational health hazards can not be overlooked. Table 2.20 presents data relating to health hazards associated with different risky occupations.

Table 2.19. Different aspects of a child's development endangered by work

1. Physical Development:	Health, Strength, Vision & Hearing.
2. Cognitive Development:	Acquisition of knowledge to lead a normal life, read write and understanding.
3. Emotional Development:	Adequate self-esteem, family attachment, feeling of love and affection.
4. Social Development:	Sense of group identity and the ability to cooperate with others.
5. Moral Development:	Capacity to distinguish between right and wrong, good and bad etc.

Table 2.20. Industrial Health Hazards

Occupation	*Type of health hazard*
Agriculture	Diseases due to pesticide/insecticide and malnutrition
Brassware	Respiratory tract infection, chronic bronchitis and bone disorder
Carpet Weaving	Peticosys, distortion in backbone, weakening eye sight, TB and skin problem
Handloom	Lungs problem, Asthma, T.B. and eye problem
Match & Fire Work	Severe back & neck pain, casualties on account of explosion
Glass& Bangles	Asthma, TB, bronchitis, chronic anaemia, skin burns, stunted growth and damage in liver and vital organs.
Gem & Diamond	TB, skin disease, eye problem, viral and urinary infection

Occupation	*Type of health hazard*
Lock	Asthma, bronchitis, TB, ear & eye problem
Bidi Industry	Chronic bronchitis and tuberculosis
Zari & embroidery	Eye defects
Construction	Stunts the growth of the child
Ragpicking	Tetanus and skin disease
Pottery	Asthma, bronchitis, tuberculosis
Stone quarries	Silicosis
Balloon Industry	Pneumonia, heart ailment and / or heart attack

Source: Archana Sinha, 1998, Social Action, 48, 1, 38; *Children of Darkness*, Manjiri Dingwani *et al.*

REFERENCES

1. Child labour, Encyclopaedia Britannica, pp. 320-321.
2. Jain, S.N., *Preventive Legal Measures in the Area of Child* Labour, National Seminar on Child labour and the Law (Unpublished), 1982, pp. 725.
3. Sikiligar, P.C., 1997, *Evaluation of Centrally-sponsored Scheme of Boys Hostel for Scheduled Castes*, NIRD, Hyderabad, Unpublished Report.
4. Myron Weiner, 1991, *The Child and the State in India: Child Labour and Education Policy in Comparative Perspective, Princeton University Press.*
5. The Annual Report 1995-96, *The National Human Rights Commission*, Government of India, New Delhi. .
6. *Child Labour: Targeting the Intolerable*. International Labour Conference (Report VI,i)-86th Session, 1998, ILO, Geneva.
7. *World of Work*, No. 23, 1998, pp. 10-11.
8. Child Labour: Targeting the Intolerable. *op. cit.*
9. *World of Work*, No. 18, 1996, pp. 7.

3

Child Labour Eradication Programme: A Bird's Eye View

Children are most valuable assets of a nation. They should be protected from all types of exploitation, ill-treatment and abuses. The future of a nation mainly banks upon the children who in their later part of life contribute to the work force, administrative set-up, and efficient productive system. The socio-economic-political set up of a country gets endangered with the use of these precious brains in an unscrupulous manner.

But it is very unfortunate to mention that child labour is an economic practice though it is a social evil. It is as old as the human civilization. It has existed in some form or the other from time immemorial. The industrial revolution of 19th century had brought a number of young children into mines and factories, where they worked long hours in dangerous and unhygienic conditions. However, long before that time children had worked hard in agriculture and in shops, where they worked for their parents. Child labour is unethical in nature, illegal in the eyes of law, immoral by any convention and illegitimate in practice.

No civilized human being with a sound mind can support child labour. Hence, it should be dealt with an iron hand. The novelist Charles Dickens and the socialist Karl Marx were among those who helped to arouse public opinion against the practice of child labour.[1] In India Raj Kapoor through Boot Ploish in 1952 and Meera Nair through *Salam Bombay* in 1992 gave us film portraits of child labour in urban slums of Mumbai. These portraits were not only heart touching but contextually accurate and insightful as well.

Child labour is not new in India. It was in existence even before 321 B.C. In most cases it was in the form of child slavery. In *Arthasastra*, Kautilya prohibited the trade of children. Kautilya during the regime of Maurays' codified rules with a spirit of abolition of child slavery. These codes were:

1. Children under 8 years of age were banned from carrying out low and ignoble works.
2. Purchase and sale of children below 8 years of age was prohibited.
3. Provisions were made to relieve oneself from slavery either paying the dues or otherwise.
4. Wages were to be paid according to time, work and / or contract made. Wages were to be settled upon before the work was actually begun.

Due to change of socio-cultural and political condition of India the practice of child labour and child slavery had a declining trend during the post-Mauriyans' era. However, in Mediaval period, particularly during Mughal kings exploitative child labour practice was at its high. It was basically due to callousness of the rulers towards the welfare of the common man, recurrence of famine and increasing population pressure.

Large-scale industry based on factory system, was introduced in India during the British Rule. Under the patronage of the East India Company certain industrial organizations grew in 18th and 19th centuries involving large scale employment in sectors like weaving, carpentry, etc. The new set of establishments yield a new socio-economic order in place of old family based farm-economy. Frequent occurrence of famine, prolonged scarcity of food, lack of education facility, absence of compulsory child education coupled with opportunity for wage-paid employment and expanded labour market had resulted in introduction of children in to labour market. Such a grim situation created a number of socio-economic problems. Employment of children at a tender age was one among those.

In the 19th century employment of children in jute and cotton mills, mines, factories and underground work grew without age bar. The condition of workers in modern factories and plantations in the 19th century was miserable. They had to work between 12 and 16 hours a day and there is no weekly day of rest. Women and children worked the same long hours as men. The wages were extremely low, ranging from Rs. 4 to Rs. 20 per month. The factories were overcrowded, badly lighted and aired, and completely unhygienic. Work on machines was hazardous, and accidents very common. Lack of state regulations regarding wages, working hours and wage limit, the child employment resulted unabated exploitation by their employers. Child labourers had been the worst sufferers. This drew the attention of the public leaders, philosophers and the social activists. The factory workers too in the country united together in 1875 for securing better working conditions in factories, especially for women and children. As a sequel to this the first Indian Factory Act came into existence in 1881.

Legislative history with respect to child labour has traversed a long path since 1881. Over the long period, the statutory provisions on child labour have concentrated mainly on a few aspects like reducing the working hours, raising the minimum age in defining a child and different activities which a child can undertake. The history of development of child labour legislation in India can be divided into two stages: pre and post independence.

Before Independence

The following Box 3.1 envisages the legislations enacted by the Government of India prior to independence.

Some of the important legislations providing legal Protection to child labour in various occupations are being discussed in detail in ensuing paragraph.

The Indian Factories Act, 1881

In spite of active opposition from the employers, the company government passed the first legislation in 1881 for protecting the interest of labourers, including child labourers. The salient provisions of this Act concerning child labour are as follows:

1. Prohibits employment of children below 7 years of age.

2. Banned employment of child in two factories on the same day.
3. Maximum working hours are 9 hours per day including rest intervals.
4. Monthly 4 holidays is a must.
5. Safety measures such as, fencing dangerous machines is a must.

Box 3.1
Legislations enacted by the Government of India Prior to Independence

1. The Indian Factories Act, 1881.
2. The Indian Factories Act, 1891.
3. The Mines Act, 1901.
4. The Factories Act, 1911.
5. Inland Steam Vessels Act, 1917
6. The Factories (Amendment) Act, 1922
7. The Indian Mines Act, 1923
8. The Factories Amendment Act, 1926
9. The Indian Port (Amendment) Act 1931
10. The Tea Districts Emigration Act, 1932
11. The Children (Pledging of Labour) Act 1933
12. The Factories Act, 1934
13. The Indian Mines (Amendment) Act, 1935
14. The Employment of Children Act, 1938

The factories act had been modified several times till 1948 on the basis of recommendations made by the Factory Commission (1948), The Freer Smith Committee (1906), the Factory Labour Commission (1907) and the Royal Commission on Labour (1929-31).

The Indian Factories Act (Revised), 1891

1. Minimum age was increased to 9 years.
2. Child means any person below 14 years of age.

3. Hours of work were limited to a maximum 7 hours per day, with prohibition of work at night between 8 p.m. and 5 a.m.

The Indian Factories Act (Revised), 1911:

1. Working hours reduced to 6 hours per day.
2. Work of children between 7 p.m. and 9.30 a.m. prohibited.
3. Work in certain dangerous processes prohibited.
4. Employer was required to submit age and fitness certificate of the child employed in his/her factory.

The Factories Amendment Act, 1922

1. Scope of the Act extended to cover all premises where the use of mechanical power is there and where 20 or more persons were employed.
2. Minimum age limit of a child increased to 15 years.
3. Maximum working hours fixed at 6 hours and half an hour interval is a must for children employed for more than 5½ hours.
4. Not to employ young person below 18 years and women in certain processes.
5. Provision for medical certificate of age and fitness plus certificate for re-examination for continuing work.

The Factories Amendment Act, 1926

This amendment imposed certain penalties on the parents and guardians for allowing their children to work in two separate factories on the same day.

The Factories Amendment Act, 1934

1. Employment of children below 12 years prohibited.
2. Children between 12 and 15 years: Employment restricted to 5 hours a day.
3. Child between 15 and 17 years is defined as adolescent who may be employed with certain restrictions.

The Mines Act, 1901

The second major legal provision for protecting the child labourers was the passing of the Mines Act in 1901. The Mines Act prohibited employment of children in mines below 12 years of age.

Indian Mines (Amendment) Act, 1923

The Mines Act, 1901 was first amended in 1923. Under this amendment:

1. The minimum age for employment of a child in mines was raised to 14 years.
2. The working hours was fixed at 54 hours per week in underground and 60 hours over ground activities.
3. The working days were restricted to 6 per week.

The Mines Amendment Act, 1935

This amendment introduced divisions of children according to age groups and the following restrictions were introduced:

1. Employment of children under 15 years in mines was prohibited.
2. Underground employment of persons between 15 and 17 years was permitted only on production of certificate of physical fitness granted by a qualified medical practitioner.
3. Working time restricted to maximum of 10 hours a day for work above the ground and 9 hours a day for work underground, however, in both the cases 54 hours per week.

Indian Ports Act, 1908

A series of legislations relating to docks and ports prohibiting employment of children had been passed since 1889. but a consolidated Act was brought out in 1908. in an amendment to this Act in 1922 the minimum age of employment in ships, ports and docks was raised to 12 years, which was further raised to 14 years in *The Indian Merchant Shipping Act* of 1923.

Tea Districts Emigrant Labour Act, 1932

1. Under this Act persons below the age of 16 years of age shall not be employed in tea gardens of Assam.
2. No child should be employed or allowed to migrate unless the child is accompanied by his parents or an adult on whom the child is dependent.

The Children (Pledging of Labour) Act, 1933

The main objective of this Act was to prevent pledging of the labour of a child, made such agreements void and stopped exploitation of children. This Act prohibited pledging of children, i.e., taking of advances by parents and guardians in return for bonds, pledging the labour of their children – system akin to that of present day bonded labour system.

1. Under the Act a person below 15 years of age was treated as a child.
2. Penalty had been fixed under the Act up to Rs 50/- for pledging / making agreement to pledge the labour of a child by the parents or guardian.
3. The Act provided that the employer was to be fined by an amount up to Rs 200 for the breach of the law.

Employment of Children Act, 1938

The objective of this Act was to prevent the evils of child employment in workshops and factories not covered by the Factories Act. This Act was passed to implement the convention adopted by the 23rd session of the ILO (1937), which inserted a special article for India, that: children under the age of 13 years shall not be employed or work in the transport of passengers, or goods, or mails or by rail or in the handling of goods at docks, but excluding transport by land. Children under the age of 15 years shall not be employed or work in occupations to which this Article applies which are scheduled as dangerous or unhealthy by the competent authority.

In its first amendment in 1939 employment of children below 12 years of age was banned in 10 processes. These are: (1) Bidi Making, (2) Carpet Weaving, (3) Cement Manufacture and Bagging of Cement, (4) Cloth Printing, Dyeing and Weaving,

(5) Manufacture of Matches, Explosives and Fireworks, (6) Mica-cutting and Splitting, (7) Shellac Manufacture, (8) Soap Manufacture, (9) Tanning, and (10) Wool Cleaning.

After Independence

India got independence in 1947. Not satisfied with the efforts put by the British Government for regulating the employment of child labour, the Government of India had further introduced several steps towards this end. The history of efforts undertaken by the Government of India in post-independent period can be divided into two parts: (1st Phase) from 1947 to 1980 and (2nd Phase) from 1980 till date.

1st Phase (1947 - 1980)

In the first phase several legislations were enacted for improving the conditions of child labour. Box 3.2 highlights the Acts passed by the Government of India to put a curb on the menace of child labour during this phase.

Box 3.2

Legislations Enacted by the Government of India after Independence

1. The Factories Act, 1948.
2. The Minimum Wages Act, 1948.
3. The Shops and Establishment Act, 1948.
4. The Employment of Children (Amendment) Act, 1949.
5. The Employment of Children (Amendment) Act, 1951.
6. The Employment of Children (Amendment) Act, 1978.
7. The Plantation Labour Act, 1951.
8. The Indian Mines (Amendment) Act, 1952.
9. The Merchant Shipping act, 1958.
10. The Apprentices Act, 1961.
11. The Motor Transport Workers Act, 1961.
12. Atomic Energy Act, 1962.
13. The Beedi and Cigar Workers (condition of Employment) Act, 1966.
14. The Contract Labour Act, 1970.
15. Bonded Labour System (Abolition) Act, 1976.

Factories Act, 1948

This Act replaced all the previous enactments on factories and raised minimum age for employment in factories to 14 years.

A young person [a child or an adolecent - Sec.2 (d)] shall not be allowed to work in a factory unless a certificate of fitness is granted with reference to him is in the custody of the manager of the factory and such young person carries a token giving a reference to such a certificate, while he is at work (Sec. 68). The Act further stated that an adolescent who has not been granted a certificate of fitness is deemed to be a child for all purposes of the Act [Sec 70(2)].

Night employment is absolutely prohibited and even day's work is restricted to 4½ hours and there can be only 2 shifts. No child can be allowed or required to work in any factory on any day on which he has already been working in another factory (Sec.71).

The manager of the factory shall maintain a register of child workers, in a prescribed manner, to be available at all times to the inspector during working hours (Sec.73) and also the manager should display at conspicuous or convenient place at or near the main entrance of the factory, a notice board showing clearly the periods of work of children for the respective days of the week (Sec, 72).

General penalty to manager and occupier for violating above provisions is 3 months imprisonment or with fine up to Rs. 2000/- or with both. If the offence continued after conviction Rs. 75 for each day on which contravention is so continued (Sec.92). But whoever knowingly uses or helps other to use a false certificate of fitness shall be punishable with one-month imprisonment or with Rs. 50 or both (Sec. 98). Finally, all those whoever are benefited by permitting a child for double employment, parents, guardians, employer or any other person, except when it is without their consent or connivance, shall be punished with fine which may extend to Rs.50 (Sec. 99).

The Factories Act 1948 was amended in 1954. This amendment included a prohibition of employment of persons under 17 years at night. 'Night' was defined as 12 consecutive hours and which included hours between 10 p.m. and 7 a.m.

The Minimum Wages Act, 1948

This Act is a landmark in the history of child labour legislation in the country. It recognized that the determination of wages can not be left to be determined by market forces, rather regulated by Minimum Wages Act, 1948. Child labour is not the organized labour, so as to compel the employer to act upon the demands made by them. The obligation has therefore been imposed on the state to see the welfare of the child employees.

The Minimum Wages Act adopted the definition and meaning assigned to the words 'adult', 'adolescent' and 'child' in Factories Act, 1948. In fixing or revising minimum rates of wages under section 3(3) of the Act:

(*a*) Different minimum rates of wages may be fixed.

- (*i*) Different scheduled employments.
- (*ii*) Different classes of work in the same scheduled employment.
- (*iii*) Adults, adolescents, children and apprentices.
- (*iv*) Different localities.

(*b*) Minimum rates of wages may be fixed by any one or more of the following wage periods.

- (*i*) By the hours
- (*ii*) By the day
- (*iii*) By the month
- (*iv*) By such other large wage periods as the case may be indicated

The act prohibits the employment of children for more than 4½ hours for any normal working day. Any employer who contravenes any provisions of this Act or of any rule or other made there under shall if no penalty is provided for such contravention by this Act be punishable with fine which may extend to Rs 500/-.

Amendment to Employment of Children Act, 1938 in 1949

The Employment of Children Act, 1938 was amended in 1949 introducing a few new provisions in it.

1. The minimum age for employment in workshops was raised from 12 to 15 years.
2. The Act also prevented the employment of children below 15 years of age in hazardous and unhealthy occupations, in occupations connected with transport of passengers and goods in railway and/or port authority.

The Act was again amended in 1951. This amendment was required as a result of the ILO convention relating to night work of young person. This amendment prohibited the employment of children between 15 and 17 years at night in railways and ports and also provided to maintain register showing their names, rest interval and date of birth for children under 17 years.

This Act has been further amended in 1978. the amendment prohibits employment of a child below 15 years in any occupation as transport of passenger, goods or mail by railway, cleaning of ash pits, cylinder picking, catering establishment at railway station, as a vendor and any other work which is carried on in close proximity to or between the railway lines. This amendment further prescribes interval of rest for 12 consecutive hours, which shall include at least seven consecutive hours between 10 p.m. and 7 a.m.

Shops and Establishments Act, 1948

This is a State Act. This Act has been committed for the benefit of workers, women and child labour employed in the shops and establishments. In addition to all the Central statute prohibiting or regulating the employment of children, various State legislatures have passed Acts, regulating the conditions of work of workers in shops and establishments. Subject to certain exceptions, these acts apply in the first instance to shops, commercial establishments, restaurants, hotels and places of amusement in certain notified urban areas. The State Governments are, however, empowered to extend the application of the Act to such other areas or to such categories of undertakings in such areas, as they may consider necessary. Time to time these Acts has been amended to meet the situation. The provisions in these Acts regulate the daily and weekly hours of work, to opening and closing hours, rest intervals, payment of wages, over-time, night work, pay, holidays with pay, annual leave, employment of children and young persons, etc. These Acts have prohibited the employment of children and regulated the work of young persons in the shops and other establishment.

The provisions from State to State vary. However, to generalize with approximation, it can be said that the difference in minimum age limits varies between 12 and 15 years. The working hours fixed for children are usually 5 per day or 30 per week, for adolescent 7 per day and 42 per week.

Section 2(2) of the Act defines 'child' as a person who has not completed his 15 years of age. Section 32 States that no child shall be required or allowed to work whether as an employer or otherwise in any establishment, if such child is a member of the family of the employer. Section 33 prohibits employment of young person to work as an employee in any establishment before 6 a.m. and 7 p.m.

Provisions Relating to Hours of Work for Young Persons in Different States in the Act

State	*Age*	*Working Hours*	*Hours of work*	*Rest Interval*
Andhra Pradesh	14-17	6 a.m. to 7 p.m.	7 per day & 42 per week, No overtime	
Bihar	12-18	7 a.m. to 7 p.m.	Children 5 per day & 30 per week. Young persons 7 per day & 42 per week	1 hour after 4 hours of continuous work
Gujarat	12-17	6 a.m. to 7 p.m.	6 per day	½ an hour after 3 hours' continuous work
Himachal Pradesh	14-20	-	5 per day & 30 per week	-Do-
Haryana	-18-20	-	5 per day & 30 per week	-Do-
J&K	12-18	7 a.m. to 9 p.m.	6 per day	-Do-
Maharashtra	12-17	6 a.m. to 7 p.m.	6 per day	-Do-
Kerala	14-17	7 a.m. to 7 p.m.	-	-Do-

State	*Age*	*Working Hours*	*Hours of work*	*Rest Interval*
Madhya Pradesh	12-17	6 a.m. to 9 p.m.	5 per day	-Do-
Karnataka	12-15	6 a.m. to 8 p.m.	5 per day	-Do-
Orissa	12-15	6 a.m. to 10 p.m.	5 per day	-Do-
Punjab	14-18	-	5 per day, 30 per week	-Do-
Rajasthan	12-15	6 a.m. to 10 p.m.	3 per day	-
Tamil Nadu	14-17	6 a.m. to 7 p.m.	7 per day, 42 per week	-
Uttar Pradesh	14-17	-	6 per day	-
West Bengal	12-15	Not after 8 p.m.	7 per day, 40 per week	1 hour after 4 hours' work

The Plantation Labour Act, 1951

This Act was passed to protect the children engaged in plantation works such as Tea, Coffee, Rubber and Cincona throughout the country except Jammu and Kashmir.

This Act prohibited employment of children under 12 years in plantation. This Act provides for the welfare of labour in plantations and regulates the conditions of work of such labour. In Clauses (a) and (c) of Section 2 the child has been redefined as a person who has not completed the age of 14 years, with the Amendment in 1986. At the same time that Amendment has struck down the minimum age which was 12 years and allowed any child below 14 years and any adolescent (below 18) to work in plantations but with a certificate of fitness, by carrying a token to this effect while at work, issued by surgeon. Such certificate is valid only for one year. However, if an inspector thinks necessary, may cause any young person employed in a plantation to be examined by certificate of fitness, by certifying surgeon. Use of a false certificate of fitness is punishable by imprisonment which may extend to one month or with fine or both (Section 34). Except with special permission from the Government or that particular state, no child or adolescent shall be required or allowed to work for more than 27 hours a week (Section 19). However, daily maximum hours are not prescribed. Section 25 says that except with the permission of the state government no child workers should be employed in any plantation between 6 p.m. to 7 a.m.

Indian Mines (Amendment) Act, 1952

The original Mines Act, 1923 was amended after India's independence in 1952 and 1983. Amendment in 1952 prohibited the employment of children under 15 years in mines. After the commencement of the Mines (Amendment) Act 1983, no person below 18 years of age shall be allowed to work in any mine or part thereof. However, sub-section (2) of this section states that apprentices and other trainees, below 16 years of age may be allowed to work with a medical certificate of fitness for work under proper supervision in a mine or part thereof by the manager. A certificate is valid only for two months. Such adolescents are allowed to work in any mine except between 6 a.m. and 6 p.m. Penalty/punishment for use of false certificate of fitness under the Act is imprisonment which, may extend to one month or with fine which may extend to Rs. 200 or with both and for employment of persons below 18 years a fine to the extent of Rs. 500 can be imposed.

The new Act permits employment of a child in underground works, if he fulfills two conditions: (1) child must have completed 18 years of age and (2) child must have a certificate of physical fitness from a medical surgeon.

The Merchant Shipping Act, 1958

No person under 15 years of age shall be engaged or carried to sea to work in any capacity in any ship, except:

1. In a school ship, or training ship in accordance with prescribed conditions; or
2. In a ship in which all persons employed are members of one family; or
3. In a home trade shipping of less than two hundred tons gross; or
4. Where such a person is to be employed on nominal wages and will be in charge of his father or other adult near male relative.

It will thus be seen that in Merchant Shipping, it is only under the direct control of parents or guardians the child can put to service. Section 111 of the Act stipulates that no young person (person under 18 years of age) can be employed as a trimmer or stocker unless he is granted a medical certificate of fitness by the competent authority. This Act imposes a fine up to Rs 50/- on any person who contravenes the provision of the Act.

The Apprentice Act, 1961

This Act has been enacted with a view to meet the increasing demand of skilled craftsman in the development of the country. This Act lays down that no person shall be qualified for being engaged as an apprentice to undergo apprenticeship training in any designated trades unless he is at least fourteen years old and satisfies such standards of education and physical fitness as may be prescribed (Section 3). In case of a minor a contract of apprenticeship has to be entered into by the guardian with the employer (Section 4). The weekly hours or work of an apprentice, while undergoing practical training shall be 42 to 48 hours. In the basic training 42 hour; Second year of apprenticeship 42 to 45 hours; and during third or subsequent year 48 hours, Provided, however, that short-term apprentices may be engaged to work up to a limit or 48 hours per week. The Act also prohibited night work of apprentice (i.e., between 10 p.m. to 6 a.m.) except in case of short-term apprentice and with the prior approval of the apprenticeship advisor who shall give his approval if he is satisfied that it is in the interest of the training of the apprentice or in the interest of public.

Penalty for engaging a person as an apprentice who is below the age of 14 years is punishable with imprisonment which may extend to 6 months or with fine or with both.

Motor Transport Workers Act, 1961

This Act prohibits employment of children below 15 years of age in any capacity in any Motor Transport undertaking. Section 22 of the Act states that no adolescent (person in 15-18 years of age) shall be required or allowed to work as a Motor Transport Worker in any Motor Transport undertaking without a certificate of fitness granted with reference to him. Such an adolescent carries with him while he is at work a token given a reference to such certificate. The provisions relating to certificate of fitness are more or less similar to other Acts.

The Act imposes a penalty of imprisonment which may extend to one month or with any fine up to Rs. 50/- or with both for the use of false certificate of fitness, but for contravention of the Act, imprisonment may extend up to 3 months so also fine to Rs. 500.

Atomic Energy Act, 1962

The Central government has made the Radiation, Protection Rules 1971 under section 30 of the Act. This Act prohibits the employment of person below the age of 18 years as radiation worker, except for the prior permission of the competent authority.

Bidi and Cigar Workers (Conditions of Employment) Act, 1966

This Act stipulates that no child (below 14 years of age) shall be required or allowed to work in any industrial premises manufacturing bidis or cigars. Section 25 of the Act prohibits the employment of women or young person (age between 14-18 years) between 7 p.m. and 6 a.m.

The normal conditions necessary for welfare of the employees are required to be provided by the employer in the industrial premises. These necessities are laid down in section 8 to 16 of the Act which are viz., cleanliness, ventilation; avoiding overcrowding by providing minimum at the rate of at least four and quarter cubic meter of space for every person employed therein, sufficient supply of wholesome drinking water at convenient and suitable points, latrines and urinals, washing facilities, crèches, first aid, canteens.

The Act specifies that no employee shall be required or allowed to work in any industrial premises for more than 9 hours in any day or for more than 48 hours in any week. However, any adult (above 18 years of age) employee may be allowed to work in such industrial premises for any period in excess of limit fixed under this section subject to payment of overtime work, does not exceed 10 hours in any day in the aggregate 54 hours in any week.

The Contract Labour Act, 1970

The 'contract labour' employed in industries, mines, plantations and docks etc. are different from the 'bonded labour'. The contract labourers are not directly recruited by the establishments, their names do not appear in the pay roll and they are not directly paid by the employer.

The National Commission on Labour (1969) observed persistence of child labour in various unorganized sectors and establishments in varying degrees. Following such report, this all India Act was passed in 1970, which covers all establishments and contractors employing 20 or more workers.

As no specific provision was made in this Contract Labour Act (1970) prohibiting child employment, so child labour had been observed in building works, construction of roads and in certain other establishments under the contractors. Thus, the main objective of the Act had failed though the system of contract labour was abolished in the country by the passing of this Act.

Bonded Labour System (Abolition) Act, 1976

Primarily the 'slavery' is the outcome of this right of individual to sell his children for his need. Although the slavery has been abolished on account of the efforts of the British rule in India, the other forms did not end. To secure the service of others at concessional and cheap rates, the Rulers and Traders invented different methods and forms. If the debtor is not able to repay his loan, he used to render services himself along with his children. Various forms prevailing in different parts of the country have been quoted in explanation to section 2(b) of the Bonded Labour System (Abolition) Act, 1976 as:

> "Agreement means an agreement, whether written or oral, or partly written and partly oral between a debtor and creditor, and includes an agreement providing for forced labour, the existence of which is presumed under any social custom prevailing in the concerned locality in relation to the following forms of forced labour, namely: Adddiyamar, Baramasia, Basahya, Bethu, Bhagela, Cherumar, Garru-Galu, Hali, Hari, Harwai, Holya, Jana, Jeetha, Kamiya, Khundit-Mundit, Kuthia, Lakhari, Munjhi, Mat, Munish

system, Nit-Majoor, Paleru, Padiyal, Pannayilal, Sagri, Sanji, Sanjawat, Sewak, Sewwakia, Seri, Vetti".

Acts at a Glance

Act	Provisions
Factories Act, 1948	* Prohibits employment of children below 14 years of age. * Restricted night employment of child. * Maximum working hour is limited to 4½ hours per day.
Minimum Wages Act	* The Act pertains to fixation of minimum wages for different category of workers, employment and location. * Normal working hour of a child should be 4½ hours a day. * Any employer who contravenes any provision/rule of this Act shall be liable for legal action/punishment.
Employment of Children Act	* Minimum age for employment in workshop was raised from 12 to 15 years. * Prescribes 12 consecutive hours of rest in a day. * The labour inspector was empowered to refer the matter to the prescribed medical officer for verification of age in case of dispute arising between the employer and himself.
Shops & Establishment Act	* Applies to hotels, restaurants, commercial establishments and places of amusement. * Prohibits the employment of children below its prescribed age. * No child is allowed to work before 6 a.m. & after 7 p.m.
Plantation Labour Act	* Prohibits employment of young children who have not completed 14 years of age. * Provides educational facilities to children between 6-12 years of age

	employed in plantation, if they exceed 25 Nos.
	* Maximum working hours was limited to 27 hours per week.
Indian Mines Act	* Minimum age of work is 18 years
	* Work is banned from 6 p.m. to 6 a.m.
Apprentice Act	* Prohibits the apprenticeship/ training of a person below 14 years of age
	* Debars the employer from training the apprentice as an employee
Motor Transport Workers Act	* Prohibits employment of children below 15 years of age
Bidi & Cigar Workers Act	* Prohibits employment of children below 14 years of age in bidi & cigar making industrial premises.
	* Prohibits overtime for young persons
	* Night work (7 p.m. to 6 a.m.) is prohibited
Contract Labour Act	* Covers all establishments and contractors employing 20 or more workers. However, no specific provision was made in this Act for prohibiting child employment.

In 1950, the constitution of independent India came in to force. The constitution makers of India incorporated important provisions for the betterment and protection of the up coming citizens, affirmed their faith on the dictum, "children are the wealth of nation". Indian constitution has affirmed the protection of the children below 14 years of age in its chapter on 'Fundamental Rights' and 'Directive Principles of State Policy'. Let us enumerate some of the important provisions of the Indian constitution dealt with this issue. Box 3.3 contains these constitutional safeguards.

Box 3.3

Constitutional Safeguards for Child laobur

Article 14: Equality before law

Article 15: Prohibition of discrimination on ground of religion, race, caste, sex or place of birth

Article 15(3): Our constitution permits the state to make special provisions to restrict the employment of children in certain areas. "Nothing in this article shall prevent the state from making any special provisions for women and children".

Article 21: Protection of life and personal liberty

"No person shall be deprived of his life or personal liberty except according to procedure established by law".

Article 23: Prohibition of traffic in human beings and forced labour

Traffic in human beings and beggar and other similar forms of forced labour are prohibited and any contravention of this provision shall be an offence punishable in accordance with law.

Article 24: Prohibition of employment of children in factories, etc

No child below the age of fourteen years shall be employed to work in any factory or mine or engaged in any other hazardous employment.

Article 39 (e) & (f): Certain principles of policy to be followed by State :

The state shall, in particular, direct its policy securing

(*e*) that the health and strength of workers, men and women, and the tender age of children are not abused and that citizens are not forced by economic necessity to enter avocations unsuited to their age or strength.

(*f*) That children are given opportunities and facilities to develop in a healthy manner and in conditions of freedom and dignity and that childhood and youth are protected against exploitation and against moral and material abandonment

Article 42: Provision for just and human conditions of work and maternity benefit

Article 43: Living wages, etc., for workers

Article 45: Provision for free and compulsory education for children

The state shall endeavour to provide, within a period of ten years from the commencement of this Constitution, for free and compulsory education for all children until they complete the age of fourteen years.

Article 47: Duty of the state to raise the level of nutrition and standard of living and to improve public health

Article 51(c): Promotion of international peace and security.

The State shall endeavour to -

(*c*) Foster respect for international law and treaty obligations in the dealings of organized people with one another.

2nd Phase (from 1980 till date)

Government of India followed a pro-active policy in the matter of tackling the problem of child labour. Several ILO conventions relating to child labour have been ratified by India. The provisions contained in the Indian Constitution and host of legislations pertaining to child labour is quite consistent with the resolution adopted at the International Labour Conference (1979). The resolution calls for a combination of prohibiting measures for humanizing child labour, wherever the same can not be eliminated in a short span of time.

The National Policy for Children Resolution was adopted in 1974. The policy resolution envisages several measures to provide adequate services to children. The policy measure includes: free and compulsory education for all children up to the age of 14 years, providing alternative forms of education of children who were unable to reap the full advantage of formal school education, provision of health and nutrition service, and to protect children against neglect, cruelty and exploitation. The policy also provides that no child under the age of 14 shall be permitted to be engaged in hazardous occupations and to undertake heavy work.

Gurupadaswamy Committee

In order to look into the causes leading to and problems arising out of employment of children and to suggest suitable measures for their protection and welfare, the Ministry of Labour, Government of India, had set up a committee headed by Sri M.S. Gurupadaswamy in 1979. The following were terms of reference of the committee.

1. Examine existing laws, their adequacy and implementations, and suggest corrective action to be taken to improve implementation and to remove defects.
2. Examine the dimensions of child labour, the occupations in which children are employed, etc. and suggest new areas where laws abolishing/regulating the employment of children can be introduced.
3. Suggest welfare measures, training and other facilities, which would be introduced to benefit children in employment.

The Committee had drawn up an action plan for in-depth study on the nature and supportive measures for working children. The committee had prepared a questionnaire to elicit information on child labour from the public, politicians, trade unions, social workers, employers, parents of child worker, Government and Non-government organizations, etc. The information so obtained had been utilized in the report. The report of the committee was submitted to the Government in December 1979.

The Committee recognized that a distinction had to be made between child labour and the exploitation of child labour because, though both are a problem, they are of different orders. It had emphasized that, in future, all action dealing with child labour has to take note of the basic aspect. Which is that "labour becomes an absolute evil in the case of the child, when he is required to work beyond his physical capacity; when the hours of employment interfere with his education, recreation and rest; when his wages are not commensurate with the quantum of work done; and when the occupation, he is engaged, endangers his health and safety".

The Committee feels that:

(*i*) Child labour is to be protected from exploitation.

(*ii*) Protection must be given to the child labour, who is subjected to work in hazardous conditions which endanger such children's physical and mental development.

(*iii*) Child labour should be ensured of safety and health at the working places.

(*iv*) Child labour should be protected from excessively long working hours and from night work.

(*v*) There should be regulated work even in non-hazardous occupations.

(*vi*) Child labour should be provided with sufficient weekly rest periods and holidays in their employments.

The Committee proposed to take certain steps to addressing the root causes of child labour. These are:

(*i*) The measures to promote employment oriented development, both in rural and urban areas.

(*ii*) The all-round development and extension of adequate facilities for both formal and non-formal education.

(*iii*) Vocational education and training.

(*iv*) The coverage and extension of social security and family welfare measure.

As per the recommendation of the Gurupadaswamy Committee, Government of India had taken certain steps as mentioned below:

(*i*) A child labour cell has been set up in 1979 under the ministry of labour.

(*ii*) A Central Advisory Board on Child Labour has been set up to advise government on the measures to be taken towards progressive elimination of child labour. It was initially constituted in March 1980 and reconstituted from time to time.

(*iii*) The Child Labour (Prohibition and Regulation) Act, 1986 has been enacted.

(*iv*) As per the requirement Child Labour Technical Advisory Committee has been constituted to advise the central government for the purpose of adding the list of occupations and process in which employment of children is prohibited.

(*v*) Dialogue has been initiated with trade unions and employers organizations to explore their co-operation in respect of the needs of working children.

(*vi*) Department of Education has set up a number of non-formal education centers with the help of voluntary organizations.

(*vii*) The recommendations of the Committee were also considered while formulating the National Child Labour Policy, 1987.

(*viii*) Financial assistance is provided to voluntary organizations for taking up action-oriented projects aimed at benefiting child labour.

Child Labour (Prohibition and Regulation) Act, 1986

The Child Labour (Prohibition and Regulation) Act, 1986 is an out come of various recommendations made by a series of committees such as National Commission on Labour (1969), Gurupadaswamy Committee (1979), and Sanat Mehta Committee (1984).

The Employment of Children Act, 1938 was repealed by the Child Labour (Prohibition and Regulation) Act, 1986. Actually the new Act has intended to extend the scope of the provisions of old Act, inasmuch as the old Act was meant for Ports and Railway Establishments in particular, whereas the present enactment is its extension to establishments, which includes shops, commercial establishments, workshops, farms, residential hotels, restaurants, etc.

The main features of the Act are:

(*i*) Prohibits the employment of children below 14 years of age in certain specified occupations and processes.

(*ii*) Seeks to regulate the conditions of work / work environment of children in employments in which they are not prohibited from working.

(*iii*) Brings about uniformity in the definition of 'child' (as a person who has not completed his 14 years of age) in the Minimum Wages Act, 1948, The Plantation Labour Act, 1951, The Merchant Shipping Act, 1958 and The Motor Transport Workers Act, 1961.

(*iv*) Empowers any person to file a complaint of the commission of an offence under the Act in any court of competent jurisdiction.

(*v*) Provides for stringent penalty for violation of provisions relating to child labour. The penalties will aply for violation of the provisions of minimum age of entry into employments in the Factories Act, 1948, The Mines Act, 1950, The Merchant Shipping Act, 1958 and The Motor Transport Workers Act, 1961.

(*vi*) The Act provides for constitution of a child labour Technical Advisory Committee for the purpose of addition of occupation / processes to the schedul under section 3 of the Act related to hazardous occupation and processes.

(*vii*) The Act stipulates that: (*a*) Period of work should not extend longer than 3 hours and should have one hour of rest before working for more than 3 hours. (*b*) A child may work a maximum of 6 hours per day including rest period and time spent in waiting for work. (*c*) No child shall be permitted to work between 7 p.m. and 8 a.m. or work overtime. (*d*) No child shall be permitted to work in two places on the same day. (*e*) Every child employed shall be allowed one day holiday per week and this day be specified and posted in the notice board.

National Policy on Child Labour, 1987

Realizing the fact that legislation alone would not be sufficient enough to tackle the problem of exploitation of child labour, the Government of India introduced a National Policy on Child Labour in 1987. A plan of action was prepared under the national policy to deal with the following situations:

(*i*) Where the children work, or are compelled to work, on a regular or continuous basis to earn a living for themselves and / or for their family.

(*ii*) Where their conditions of work result in their being severely disadvantaged and exploited.

(*iii*) Where abuses connected with such factors resulting on wage-employed children.

The action plan shall follow a multi-pronged strategy for ameliorating the conditions of child labour. The action plan under the National Child Labour Policy comprises:

1. The legislative action plan
2. The focusing of general development programmers for benefiting child labour wherever possible.
3. Project-based plan of action in areas of high concentration of child labour engaged in wage / quasi-wage employment.

• **Legal action plan:** This policy envisages strict enforcement of the provisions of the Child Labour (Prohibition and Regulation) Act, 1986 and other child related legislations. To ensure that children are not employed in hazardous employments, and that the working conditions of children working in non-hazardous areas are regulated in accordance with the provisions of the Child Labour Act. It also entails further identification of additional occupations and processes, which are detrimental to the health and safety of children.

• **Focus on general development programs benefiting children wherever possible:** The policy envisages the development of an extensive system of non-formal education for working children withdrawn form work and increasing the provision for employment and income generation schemes meant for their parents. A special cell – Child Labour Cell - was constituted to encourage voluntary organizations to take up activities like non-formal education, vocational training, provisions of health care, nutrition (under *ICDS scheme*), poverty eradication and education for working children.

• **Area specific projects:** To focus on areas known to have high concentration of child labour and to adopt a project approach for identification, withdrawal and rehabilitation of working children.

Task Force on Child Labour

A Task force on Child Labour has been set-up on the recommendation of the Central Advisory Board on Child Labour Under the Chairmanship of Dr. L.M.Singhvi to recommend the institutions and mechanisms necessary for implementing the Child Labour (Prohibition and Regulation) Act 1986 and Legal Action Plan contained in the National Child Labour Policy. The Task Force submitted its report in December 1989. The recommendations are grouped into three heads, viz., (1) General Recommendation, (2) Recommendation on the Child Labour (Prohibition and Regulation) Act, 1986 and (3) Recommendation on the National Policy on child Labour.

National Child Labour Project

In pursuance to the National Policy on Child Labour in 1988, the National Child Labour Project (NCLP) scheme was launched in 9 districts of high child labour endemicity in the country.

The NCLPs are area specific, time bound, and participative in as much as they involve government and non-government agencies and the community in an integrated manner. While fully recognizing the desirability of simultaneous withdrawal and rehabilitation of all working children, due to various administrative, logistic and financial reasons, a gradual and progressive approach is being adopted. This approach places priority on withdrawal and rehabilitation of children engaged in hazardous employments.

The strategy of the NCLPs is to implement model programs consisting of key elements, such as:

- Stepping up the enforcement of the prohibition of child labour.
- Providing employment to parents of working children.

- Expanding formal and non-formal education.
- Promoting school enrolment through various incentives, such as payment of stipend.
- Raising public awareness.
- Survey and evaluation

The scheme envisages running of special schools for child labour withdrawn from work. In the special schools, these children are provided formal / non-formal education along with vocational training, a stipend of Rs. 100 per month, supplementary nutrition and regular health check ups so as to prepare them to join regular mainstream schools. Under the scheme, funds are given to the District Collectors for running special schools for child labour. Most of these schools are run by the NGOs in the district. The coverage of the NCLP Scheme has increased from 12 districts in 1988 to 100 districts in Ninth Plan to 250 districts during the Tenth Plan.

The National Authority for the Elimination of Child Labour

In tune with the declaration of the Prime Minister in his Address to the Nation from Red Fort on the occasion of Independence Day, The National Authority for the Elimination of Child Labour (NAECL) was set up in September 1994. Secretaries of the Government in charge of Labour, Education, Women and Child Development, Welfare, Health and Family Welfare, Rural Development, Textiles, Finance and information & Broadcasting are members of the NAECL.

The objectives of the NAECL are:

- to lay down policies and programs for elimination of child labour, particularly in hazardous employments;
- to monitor progress of implementation of programme, projects and schemes for elimination of child labour; and
- to coordinate child-related programmes implemented by various Ministries of the Government of India to secure convergence of services.

With the setting up of the high-powered National Authority for the Elimination of Child Labour (NAECL) under the

Chairmanship of the Union Labour Minister, a convergence of services and schemes with specific focus on child labour is sought to be achieved. The composition of the NAECL - With representatives from 10 Ministries - fulfils a long-felt need for an umbrella organization to coordinate the efforts of the different arms of the Government for the sequential and progressive elimination of child labour.

National Resource Center on Child Labour

To finalize a concrete plan of action for the implementation of the directions of the Supreme Court on withdrawal and rehabilitation of working children, a Child Labour Cell has been setup in V.V. Giri National Labour Institute (VVGNLI) in 1990 with the assistance of Government of India and UNICEF. Later on the cell was upgraded into the National Resource Center on Child Labour (NRCCL). The NRCCL was set up in March 1993 with financial Support from the Ministry of Labour.

The NRCCL's objectives are to assist national and state governments, NGOs, policy makers, legislators and social groups through a variety of interventions. The NRCCL has conducted several important workshops for sharing knowledge and information and deciding the modality and the course of action on specific issues. These workshops have helped to evolve new and innovative programmes and actions. The Center has also conducted workshops for district collectors, project directors, representatives of state labour institutes, trade unions, NGOs, labour and factory inspectors, film makers, etc., on the issue of child labour.

The NRCCL has built up an impressive database on child labour and is now assisting the Ministry of Labour in the implementation of child labour programmes. Research and training are two other important activities of the NRCCL. The focus of the research projects of the Center has been on updating and upgrading the existing information as well as exploring new aspects related to child labour.

The NRCCL has trained about 1500 participants. These participants are Labour Administrators and Labour Enforcement Officers of Central and State Governments, NGO activists, trade union leaders, parents of working children, resource personnel of collaborative labour institutes and personnel of funding agencies. These training programmes are aimed at bringing about attitudinal changes among the trainees and raising their motivational level in order to enhance their capacity to fulfil the task of implementing child labour projects.

Training of trainers is another important activity of the national Resource Center on Child Labour. The endeavour is to create a large pool of trainers to extend the geographical coverage of child labour related training programmes. Meticulously designed, these training programmes endeavour to meet the requirements of different groups of trainers. Special emphasis is on sensitizing them with the problem of child labour so as to induce attitudinal change thus enabling them to play the role of catalysts. The NRCCL has recently conducted programmes to train District Collectors and project directors of all child labour endemic districts to carry out the survey and awareness generation in a cost effective and time bound manner under the National Child Labour Projects.

Dissemination of information through its numerous publications is yet another activity of NRCCL. It also provides technical support services to various agencies engaged in the tasks of implementation of child labour projects.

Besides collaborating with ILO, UNICEF and various State Labour Institutes, the NRCCL has established a network with about 400 NGOs and is assisting them in various ways in implementing child labour programmes.

Externally Funded Programmes

To supplement the governmental initiatives at the national level, international donor agencies came forward to support two parallel programmes in 1992: (*a*) International Programmer on the Elimination of Child Labour (IPEC) and (*b*) the Child Labour Action Support Programme (CLASP).

These programmes are intended to build the capacity of governmental and non-governmental agencies and the human resource development of their functionaries. The International Labour Organization implements these programmes under the overall guidance and supervision of national level steering Committees headed by the Union Labour Secretary. The steering committees have representatives of government and non-governmental organizations.

International Programme on the Elimination of Child Labour

In 1992 india became the first country to sign an MOU with the ILO to implement International Programme on the Elimination of Child Labour (IPEC) as a supplement to its National Child Labour Project.

IPEC's goals in India were to:

- Strengthen the capacity of government, employers' and workers' organizations, and NGOs to develop and implement measures geared towards the elimination of child labour;
- Withdraw children from hazardous work and provide them with alternatives; and
- Improve working conditions where immediate withdrawl from work was not possible.

To this end, IPEC supported 175 action programmes over the last decade. Two large scale projects during this period were the Integrated Area Specific Projects and the Andhra Pradesh State Based Project against Child Labour. IPEC strategy in India moved from the sporadic work of earlier years with NGOs to a more integrated approach that covered entire districts and states.

Child Labour Action Support Programme

The Government of German aided the Child Labour Action Support Programme (CLASP). It aimed at strengthening the capability of agencies implementing child labour programme. Assistance taken under this programme has been used for the purpose of supporting on-going activities under the National Policy on Child Labour.

INDUS Project

A new project was launched since 16.02.2004. This is named as Indo US Matching Grant Project (renamed as INDUS project).

The Government and the Ministry of Labour & Employment in particular, are rather serious in their efforts to fight and succeed in this direction. The number of districts covered under the NCLP Scheme has been increased from 100 to 250. In addition, 21 districts have been covered under INDUS, a similar Scheme for rehabilitation of child labour in cooperation with US Department of Labour.

Employment of Children as Domestic Servants and in *Dhabas* Banned

As per the recommendation of the Technical Advisory Committee on Child Labour headed by the Director general, ICMR, the government has decided to prohibit employment of children as domestic servants or servants or in dhabas (roadside eateries), restaurants, hotels, motels, teashops, resorts, spas or in other recreational centers. The ban has been imposed under the Child Labour (Prohibition & Regulation) Act, 1986 and has been effective since 10th October 2006. The Ministry of Labour has issued notification to this effect. The ministry has warned that anyone employing children in these categories would be liable for prosecution and other panel action under the Act.

During 1990s several declarations were adopted in various international conference to uphold the dignity and respect of the child rights. These are listed below :

- 1990 World Summit for Children and the world declaration on the survival, protection and development of children.
- 1990 World Conference on Education for All
- 1995 Conference of Labour Ministers of non-aligned countries and the declaration that was adopted at the close of the conference
- The Stockholm Congress on Commercial sexual exploitation of children held in August 1996
- The third SAARC Ministerial Conference on the Children of South Asia in August 1996 and the Declaration for

eliminating bonded child labour by the year 2000 with total elimination of child labour in the region by 2010

- The declaration adopted at the close of the two day international Conference held at Amsterdam in February 1997 (25-26 February 1997)
- The declaration and the action programmer adopted at the close of the four-day international Conference held at Oslo between 27th and 30th October 1997.

REFERENCE

1. Child labour, *Encyclopaedia Britannica*, pp. 320-321.

4
Empirical Investigation

Socio-Economic Profile of the Study Area

The district of Boudh-Kandhamal was formed on 1st January, 1948 later on this district was called as Phulbani. After 1-4-1994 with the creation of Boudh district, the popularly known Phulbani district has been renamed as the Kandhamal district, aptly so because this mountain terrain is mainly inhabited by '*kandhas*' - the aboriginal tribal of the locality.

Location

The district of Kandhamal is a centrally located district and lies in between 83° 30' to 84° 35' East longitudes and 19° 34' to 20° 34' North latitudes. It is situated 1300 meters above the sea level and is surrounded by Kalahandi and Rayagada districts in the west, Nayagarh and Ganjam districts in the east, Ganjam, Gajapati and Rayagada districts in the south and Boudh disrict in the north.[1] The total geographical area of the district is 8021 square km and constitutes 4.91 per cent of the State's total geographical area. The total forest area of the state is 5709.83 sq. km out of which Reserve forest cover is 2010 sq. km Demarcated Protected forest area is 1785.36 sq. km and 1914.47 sq. km of forest area is under Revenue department.[2] This district is a land of forests, mountains and full of scenic beauties. The district is famous for its' various tourist spots viz., putudi for waterfalls, Balaskumpa for the temple of Goddess Barala Devi, Belghar for wildlife (especially trumpeting tuskers), Chakapadh for temple of Birupaksha and Daringibadi - the Kashmir of Orissa for scenic beauty.

Climate and Rainfall

The climate of kandhamal district is sub-tropical, hot and dry in summer, dry and cold in winter. The temperature varies from a minimum of 0° Celsius to maximum of 45° Celsius. The lowest temperature in the district is felt during December and January and then it goes on increasing up to May. The average annual rainfall for the district is recorded at 1600 mm. The quantity of rainfall would have been adequate for good kharif crop but due to its uneven distribution during different seasons the district often faces drought conditions. As the major portion of land of this district is situated with altitudes varying from 1600' to 3000' above sea level the assured irrigation facility is almost negligible. However, the district is free from flood.

Demographic Features

According to 2001 census the total population of the district is 6,48,201 of which male constitutes 49.8 per cent i.e., 3,22,799 and female 50.2 per cent i.e., 3,25,402. Hence the sex ratio is infavour of female. It is 1008.[3] Most of the people of Kandhamal reside in rural area. It is 93.20 per cent in the district. Kandhamal district has the distinction of having 52 per cent of total population as Scheduled Tribe and 17 per cent as Scheduled Caste. Thirty-nine per cent of the total population is in the age group of 0 to 14 years. 47.24 per cent are termed as workers. Out of a total 3,06,209 workers 1,76,128 are main workers and rest 1,30,081 are marginal workers. The density of the district is 81 people per sq. km.

Administrative Set Up

The 2001 Census collected information from 145676 households of Kandhamal district. These households are spread over a total of 2546 revenue villages, out of which 167 are uninhabited. All these villages are clubbed into 153 Gram Panchayats. There are 12 Blocks and 2 Notified Area Councils (NACs) functioning in the district. For administrative purpose the district is divided into four Tahasils. They are G.Udayagir,

Balliguda, Daringibadi and Phullbani and two Sub-Divisions are Balliguda and Phulbani. Three members are elected by the people of G. Udayagiri, Balliguda and Phulbani constituencies to represent the district in the Orissa Legislative Assembly.[4]

Agriculture

The main economic activity of the tribal population of kandhamal is cultivation. Though they grow paddy, minor millets and maize, turmeric and ginger are their main items of cultivation. Many of them do not have agricultural land. They depend upon shifting cultivation, which is popularly known as '*podu*' cultivation.[5] Mostly the tribals practise Podu cultivation in hill slopes. Due to lack of sufficient arable lands and ploughing equipments the 'Kondha' tribes are habituated in podu cultivation. This is a labourious, dangerous and wasteful procedure of cultivation. Usually crops like 'Harada' , 'Biri', 'Kandula' and minor millets are cultivated under 'podu' cultivation.

The total cultivated (tilling) area of the district is 7650 sq. km and the paddy area constitutes around 73 per cent. Only 14.5 per cent of the cultivated lands get irrigation facilities from all available sources. The farmers depend mainly on nature/ monsoon for agriculture activities. Most of the agricultural workers belong to depressed classes, who have been neglected for ages. Average size of operational holding is 1.27 (as per 1995 census). Consumption of fertilizer is very low i.e., 4 kg /ha as against the state average of 42 kg / ha. The land productivity in the district is also low. This is on account of lack of irrigation facility, low level of soil fertility, traditional methods of cultivation, uneconomic size of land holding and inadequate credit and marketing facilities.

Collection of forest products is another important economic activity of the people of Kandhamal. The per centage of forest cover in the district with reference to states is 9.82 - highest in the State.

The following table shows the number of workers- main and marginal by sex as per 2001 census.

Table 4.1. Total Number of Workers by sex in Kandhamal

Category	*Male*	*Female*	*Total*
Main Worker	132541	43587	176128
Marginal Worker	36355	93726	130081
Total Worker	168896	137313	306209
Non Worker	153903	188089	341992

Note: 2001 census (provisional)
Source: District statistical Handbook, Kandhamal, 2005,Government of Orissa.

Table 4.2 depicts the occupational distribution of workers of kandhamal district. It is revealed that about 70 per cent of the workers are cultivators and agricultural labourers. About seven per cent of work force depends upon cottage, household and other small-scale industries. Lack of non-agricultural occupation in rural areas is highly responsible for low wages and poor economic conditions of the cultivators and agricultural labourers. Under-employment and unemployment are also responsible for low income and poor living standards of the people of kandhamal.

Table 4.2. Activitywise classification of workers in Kandhamal

Category	*Per cent*
Cultivators	33.45
Agricultural Labourers	36.01
Household Industries	7.05
Others	23.49
Total	100.00

Source: District Statistical Hand book, Kandhamal, 2005, Government of Orissa.

Industry

Kandhamal district is one of the industrially backward districts of Orissa. Industrial base of the district is very weak. It is due to the absence of adequate supply of minerals and lack of infrastructure facilities. This leads to the non-existences of large and medium scale industry. The district suffers from the absence of potential or capable entrepreneurship. Further the district has been unattractive to the outside investors/ producers due to the paucity of modern amenities.

So far as household industries are concerned the main items include handlooms, carpentry, black-smithy, pottery, fiber rope making and mat weaving. The cottage industries of significance are hill-broom making in Balliguda, Tumudibandha and Kotagarh blocks and siali leaf plate making in Tikabli and Chakapad block.

Trade and Commerce

Marketing of minor forest produce and surplus agricultural produce constitutes a pivotal position for the economic development of Tribals. Unless the producers obtain fair and remunerative return all the developmental efforts are in vein. If the exploitative middlemen continues to deny the fruits of their labour, mere pouring of funds for tribal welfare plan may not able to ameliorate the economic conditions of the rural tribal people of Kandhamal. Hence marketing and storage of agricultural produce is significant.

The local inhabitants being not quite enterprising, the over all trade and commercial activities of the district are handled by the businessmen from neighboring districts. Almost all the articles of daily consumption like rice, wheat, salt, kerosene, textile and vegetables are imported into the district. The main export items are timber, turmeric, tamarind and minor forest products. It has been observed that the Government institutions mostly consisting of the co-operatives such as AMCS, TDCC, RMCS, etc., have been able to procure a very negligible amount of the total marketable forest and agricultural produces. Middlemen still continues a dominant role in the storage and marketing of the district. It is also found that there has been a very wide and erratic fluctuation in collection of tribal products by government agencies.[6] Middlemen are still advantageous in marketing management. Farmers are acquiescent in the bargaining for pricing of their crops. Distress sale is a frequent occurrence. Farmers have to sell out their vegetables to the middlemen because these are perishable in nature.

Banking

Each of 12 blocks of the district has at least one branch of commercial bank. As on 31st March 2004 different commercial banks opened 28 branches in the district, the largest number being the State Bank of India. The government has also notified to extend the operational jurisdiction of kalahandi Gramya Bank to Kandhamal district. Eighth branches of RRBs are operating in the district as reported by 31st March 2004. A branch of Orissa State Financial Corporation also operates at Phulbani to cater to the credit needs of the industrial sector. The major sources of agricultural credit in the district are co-operative institutions, government sources and indigenous sector. The institutional agencies of rural credit have not achieved much success in the district.

Electricity and Transportation

By the end of 2001 only 1149 villages have been electrified. It turns out to be 49 per cent of the total village of the district which are electrified as against the state average of 77 per cent.

The district is entirely out of the railway map of the country. Road communication in the district is inadequate and ill maintained. No National High Way passes through the district. By the end of 2001, State high way is 389 km. The district has 5651 km Grampanchyat Roads, 532 km. P.S. Roads and 853 km village roads. Major district roads and other district roads are 133 km and 63 km respectively. Lack of adequate transport facilities has been the chief obstacle for the rapid economic development of the district.

Health

To provide medical facility to the people of Kandhamal government opened 58 Allopathic medical institutions 19 Homoeopathic dispensaries and 17 Ayurvedic institutions in the district. To provide immunization to the children DPT / Polio vaccination occurs regularly by the Department of Health and Family Welfare in the district. Effort is on to combat Malaria disease in the tribal area.

Education

The district is educationally very backward, female literacy rate is extremely low, i.e., 35.86 per cent and male literacy rate is not so high as it is 69.79 per cent. 1391 primary schools are operating in the district to meet the educational requirement of 1,11,846 students. Only 262 middle schools provide education in the district. 32,048 students have enrolled their names in these schools. As many as 100 secondary schools have been imparting education to 17,651 pupils. 15 colleges including two under Government sector are functioning in the district to spread higher education.[7] Following table reflects the educational situation of the district vis-à-vis the state.

Table 4.3. Enrolment / Out of School Children in the District

District/ State	*Enrolment (6-14 ages)*			*Out of School (6-14 ages)*			
	Boys	*Girls*	*Total*	*Boys*	*Girls*	*Total*	*Per cent*
Kandhamal	75230	70931	146161	2503	2652	5195	3.41
Orissa	3388648	3188249	6576897	136339	134444	270783	3.95

Source: www.opepa.in

From above table it can safely be concluded that Kandhmal district is predominantly an agrarian economy inhabited by poor, illiterates, unskilled, rural populations mostly belonging to Scheduled Caste and Tribe communities. Poverty and educational deprivation co-exist notwithstanding several development programmes being put into operation through three tiers Panchayati Raj System.

Empirical Investigation of the Child Labour in the District

To study the problem of child labour in Kandhmal district a case study is undertaken by the researcher. The detail methodology of the study is already mentioned in the introductory chapter. A well-structured, pre-tested questionnaire is prepared towards this end and appended in the report. The questionnaire is administered among 140 child workers and their parents; spread over 12 Grama Panchayatas and 2 NACs of Kandhamal district. The following results are obtained from this empirical investigation conducted by the research scholar.

The first section of the questionnaire deals with the queries related to the problem of the child labour to be responded by himself. The results so obtained are discussed in the coming paragraphs.

Most of the respondents are female child workers - out of 140 respondents 83 are female and rest 57 are male. In per centage basis female constitutes 59.3 per cent and male 40.7 per cent. This is mainly due to less importance on female child education. The following table represents this.

Table 4.4. Sex-wise distribution of Sample Child Labour

Sex	*Frequency*	*Percentage*
Male	57	40.7
Female	83	59.3
Total	140	100.0

Source: Computed.

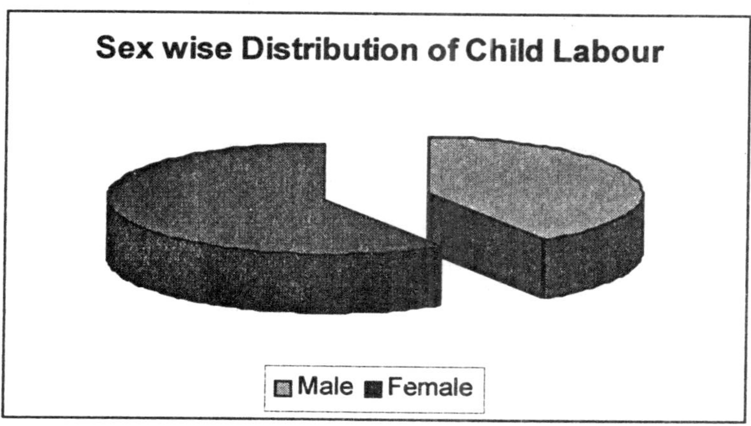

While asking about the age, their responses are as given in table 5.18. About half of the total child labour belongs to the age group of 12-14 years, twenty seven per cent belong to the age group of 9-11 years and rest is in the age group of 6-8 years. This is probably due to preference of employer for the older children. Younger children, i.e., 6-11 years old, are not physically strong enough to do the work properly.

Table 4.5. Age Structure of the Sample Child Workers

Sex	*6-8*	*9-11*	*12-14*	*Total*
Male	7	14	36	57
Female	20	24	39	83
Total	27(19.3)	38(27.1)	75(53.6)	140(100)

Source: Computed; Note: Data in parentheses shows per centage.

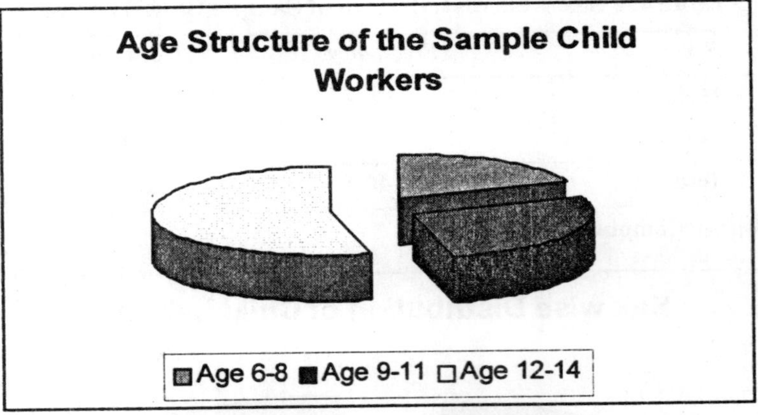

Regarding education standard of the child workers the study reveals that 79 workers are educated above 7th standard, 33 are within Class 4th to 6th rest are having education standard below 3rd. The following table reflects this fact.

Table 4.6. Education Standard of Sample Child Labour

Education standard	*Frequency*	*Percentage*
Up to standard 3rd	28	20.0
Class 4th to class 6th	33	23.6
Above 7th standard	79	56.4
Total	140	100

Source: Computed.

Asking about the activity where the child is engaged the respondents said that the following is the list of different activities where they have been employed.

1. Maid Servant: Female child workers are generally employed in this activity. Maid servants are mainly employed to perform different household activities such as cleaning of the house, cloths, utensils, cooking of the food, taking care of infants, supply of water, etc. In poor families young girls often do household chores so their mothers can work elsewhere. But girls also work often as domestic servants in rich families. Some children engaged as labourers in the neighbours' house, some others are engaged in their own house to complement or support their elder members. Very often their father and mother engaged as worker outside the house. Hence these children are entrusted with the task of domestic work as well as care takers of their younger brothers and sisters. However, in both the cases, either inside or outside the house, they have been restrained from their childhood. They are deprived of education, hence, these fellows are considered as child labourers.

2. Firewood and other forest product collection: Some of the children are engaged in the collection of firewood and other minor forest products. As forest is in close vicinity of the village in Kandhmal district people depend on forest for their livelihood to a great extent. People collect forest products such as Tamarind, Hill brooms, Myrobalan, Siali leaves, Tendu leaves, Harda, Amla, Marking nut, Soap nut, Gendigulum, Chargum, Babul / Other gum, Honey, Lac, Mahuwa Flower, Kara seed, etc., from the forest. Another important item is the firewood and coal (Angara). The preparation and marketing of 'Angara' is very often requires engagement of child labour. Some times children are employed to do these activities independently and some other time they are required as a helper to their parents for extending their helping hand. In the process they are dragged into the band of child workers.

3. Siali Khalli Stitching: Siali khalli stitching is one of the house hold / cottage industries of kandhmal district. In this industry almost all the family members are engaged, particularly the females. Children are employed to collect Siali leaves from the forest, stitching of 'Khali', 'Tunga' and supply of these articles to nearest shops, hotels, etc., Boys are engaged for collection of leaves and supply of articles whereas girls are employed for stitching.

4. Cowboy: A good number of children particularly boys are engaged as cowboy for taking care of cows, bullocks, goats, etc., They are entrusted with the task of feeding, grazing and cleaning of domestic animals. Milking of cows and marketing of milk are some other additional activities performed by the minors of the family.

5. Agricultural Labours: As most of the families of the district depend on agriculture very often children of these families are engaged in agricultural activities. Children are asked to take the meal / tiffin of their parents to the work site, go round the bullock for harvesting, cleaning of the bullocks, grazing of animals and preparation of diet for the domestic animal, collection of grass, cleaning of cow-dung and animal shade, etc. Even the regular students are also dropped during rainy season while agricultural activities are undertaken at a full swing.

6. Chips making: Crusher unit is non-existent in Kandhmaal district. So people, for chips, depend on manual preparation. In this activity both boys and girls are employed for preparation of chips out of big stones. Actually this activity is very dangerous both from physical and hygenical point of view. However, this is a cheap method for collection of money, as no investment is required for the purchase of raw materials and implements. Kandhmal district is full of hills. Therefore collection of stone is neither a difficult job nor a costly one. It costs nothing. So, poor fellows adopt this method for earning of money. In the process children below 14 years could easily be employed. Though the activity is not enlisted as a hazardous activity but it is as hazardous as the crusher units.

7. Household industry: The existence of household industries like Bamboo work, Black smithy and pottery also responsible for the continuation of child labour. Children are engaged in bamboo work for cutting, knitting and marketing bamboo articles. In the pottery industry children are employed for the collection of firewood, preparation of mud and marketing of earthen pots. Boys are also employed for running of blowing machine in the Black smith activity. Further in all theses activities small children have obtained the training to pursue the traditional family works in future. Hence, very often these activities are considered as a process of socialization of children in the family occupation.

8. Brick Making: In modern age construction of house, building and concrete work is an ever-expanding activity. For this brick is an important item. Bricks are generally made during summer season. Children are employed in brick making industry along with their family members. Children are employed for, preparation of mud, counting of bricks, arrangement of bricks and dry the brick under sun ray.

9. Hotel Boy: Hotels, restaurants, shops are some other places where we find the employment of children. Children are employed to perform the duty of adults. In hotels and restaurants boys as well as girls are engaged for doing the odd jobs, such as cleaning of utensils, plates, glasses, dining tables etc. sweeping of flours, supply of water, cutting the vegetables etc. Similarly in shops and business establishments they are asked to supply the items as desired by the customers. They work from 7 o'clock morning to 10 o'clock night. They take their fooding and bathing there without enjoying any leisure. They are available for work round the clock.

10. Motor Garage: Motor garage is another important place where we find the employment of child labour. These labourers are employed to assist the main workers. They are entrusted with the task of cleaning the motor vehicle and greasing & oiling of the vehicles.

10. Foot Path Vendor/Newspaper Vendor: Children employed themselves as vendors in the footpath. A few of them work as newspaper vendor. Footpath vendors generally trade various daily consumption / daily use goods like vegetable, ready-made garments, chapels, etc.

In the present study the distribution of child labour in different occupations are as reported in Table 4.7.

Table 4.7. Occupational Distribution of Sample Child Laboures

Occupation	*Frequency*	*Percentage*
Maid servant	29	20.7
Firewood collection	13	9.3
Khalli stitching	9	6.4
Cowboy	11	7.9
Agricultural labourer	18	12.9
Chips making	12	8.6
Household Industry	5	3.6
Motor Garage	7	5.0
Hotel boy/ shop boy	19	13.6
Brick making	9	6.4
Foot-path/ News paper vendor	8	5.6
Total	140	100

Source: Computed

In response to a query about the nature of employment except the girls employed as maid servants all other reported on daily wagers.

When they are asked about the job satisfaction 27 of them reported 'yes', 49 answered 'no' and rest either told 'cannot say' or remained 'indifferent' in their attitude (Table 4.8).

Table 4.8. Job Satisfaction of the Working Children

	Frequency	*Percentage*
Yes	27	19.3
No	49	35.0
Indifferent	64	45.7
Total	140	100

Source: Computed

When children are asked about the working hours per day in their work place, their responses are as follow:

Table 4.9. Working hours per day

Working hours	*Frequency*	*Percentage*
Less then 4 hours	31	22.1
4 to 8 hours	61	42.6
More than 8 hours	48	34.3

Source: Computed

Children who are employed as maid servant and hotel boys / shop boys acknowledged that they have been working form early in the morning to the evening 7 o'clock. Regarding remuneration the child workers reply that they have been paid very small amount as daily wage. Only hotel boys/shop boys and boys engaged in motor garage have been getting a higher wage. The following table shows the response of child workers in this regard.

Table 4.10. Remuneration of the Child Workers

Remuneration (In Rupees)	*Frequency*	*Percentage*
Less than Rs. 5	71	50.7
Rs 5 to Rs. 10	47	33.6
More than Rs. 10	22	15.7

Source: Computed.

All most all the child workers are employed in a walk-able distance from their home. Hence, they need not require any accommodation in the workplace. However, their employer generally provides the medical facility, if any problem arises at the work side (Table 4.11).

Table 4.11. Treatment at the Work Site

Responses	*Frequency*	*Percentage*
Physically abused	31	22.1
Psychologically abused	26	18.6
Not ready to respond	83	59.3

Source: Computed.

In response to the question of treatment in the field of work by their employer and fellow adults, the respondents pointed out that they are very often ill treated. But most of the children are not ready to respond with the fear that they may be put in trouble in future.

The second part of the questionnaire deals with the socio-economic setup of the child labour. It connotes the family background in which he has been brought up.

In response to the size of the family most respondents said that they have a large size family. However, all most all have nucleus family system. Seventeen respondents have lost either the father or the mother at the time of their schooling. Hence, the burden of the family is shared by the elder members of the family. The following table (Tanle 4.12) explains the size of the family of sample child workers.

Table 4.12. Size of the Family of Sample Child Worker

No. of the family members	*Frequency*	*Percentage*
1-4	22	15.7
5-8	45	32.2
9 and above	73	52.1
Total	140	100

Source: Computed.

So far as educational standard of the parent is concerned their reply is as follow (Table 4.13).

Table 4.13. Educational Standard of the Parents

Educational standard	*Father*	*Mother*
Illiterate	17 (12.1)	33 (23.6)
Below 5th stand	39 (27.9)	51 (26.4)
5th to 10th stand	78 (55.7)	56 (40.0)
Above 10th stand	6 (4.3)	0 (0.0)
Total	140 (100)	140 (100.0)

Source: Computed.
Note: Figures in parentheses represent per centage.

The respondents have further rejoined that they have been brought up in a family suffering from abject poverty. All the families are living Below Poverty Line. No one has claimed that either the father or the mother is a government servant. Regarding the occupation of the father and mother their answers are presented in Table 4.14.

Table 4.14. Occupational Distribution of the Parents

Occupation	*Father*	*Mother*
Own occupation	44 (31.4)	53 (37.9)
Daily wage	87 (62.1)	82 (58.6)
Monthly wage earner (in Pvt. Sector)	09 (6.5)	05 (3.5)
Government servant	0	0

Source: Computed.
Note: Figures in parentheses represent per centage

The incomes of these families are very low. This is clear from the household gadgets the family possesses. Rice and Dal is the main item of consumption. Fish, meat, egg are consumed only in festive occasion. Most of the houses are thatched. The houses are not equipped with facility of latrine. For drinking water the poor families depend mostly on tube well and community well. Table 4.15 explains the dependence of families for drinking water on various sources.

Table 4.15. Sources of Drinking Water

Source	*Frequency*	*Percentage*
Own well	03	2.1
Community well	88	62.9
Tube well	32	22.9
Pond/ Chuan	17	12.1
Total	140	100

Source: Computed

The last question deals with the awareness of the parents. This question deals with 10 aspects of the social life. The responses of the parents are enumerated in Table 4.16.

Table 4.16. Parents' Awareness about Social Facts

Parents awareness	*Yes*	*No*
Primary schooling is compulsory	47 (33.6)	93 (66.4)
Minimum age of work	18 (12.9)	122 (87.1)
Minimum age of marriage	15 (10.7)	125 (89.3)
Supply of mid-day meal in school	81 (57.9)	59 (42.1)
Supply of books in free of cost	105 (75.0)	35 (25.0)
Supply of school dress in free cost	45 (32.1)	95 (67.9)
About the existence of triblal residential school	29 (20.7)	111 (79.3)
Immunization facilitation	52 (37.1)	88 (62.9)
Pre-natal and post-natal service	50 (35.7)	90 (64.3)
What is child labor	12 (8.6)	128 (91.4)

Source: Computed
Note: Figures in parentheses shows per cent.

The above table explains poor social awareness of the parents living in rural area. The poor economic condition coupled with large size of the family and low social awareness are the main reasons of continuation of child labour in Kandhmal district.

REFERENCES

1. *District Statistical Handbook*, Kandhamal, 2005, Directorate of Economics & Statistics, Orissa.
2. Collectorate Kandhamal, Phulbani.
3. *Census of India, 2001*, Census Directorate, Orissa.
4. *District Statistical Handbook*, Kandhamal, 2005, Directorate of Economics & Statistics, Orissa.
5. *Annual Administrative Report 1980-81 & 1981-82*, DRDA Phulbani.
6. Satapathy, T, 1985, Marketing Strategy in Tribal Development Planning in Orissa: An Appraisal, *Orissa Economic Journal*, Vol xviii, pp. 71.
7. *District Statistical Handbook, Kandhamal*, 2005, Directorate of Economics & Statistics, Orissa.

5
Summing Up

"The child is a soul with a being, a nature and capacities of its own, who must be helped to find them, to grow into their maturity, into a fullness of physical and vital energy and the utmost breadth, depth and height of its emotional, intellectual and spiritual being; otherwise there cannot be a healthy growth of the nation".

— Justice P.N.Bhagawati, Former Chief Justice of India

Conclusions

In spite of the efforts made by the Government of India and International organizations to curb the participation of the children in the labour market, child labour continues to prevail. Millions of families living below the poverty line have to deploy their children in the labour market for their livelihood. Despite their willingness many parents find it difficult to educate their children either on account of lack of infrastructural facilities or due to abject poverty.

Kandhmal district is predominantly an agrarian economy inhabited by poor, illiterates, unskilled, rural population mostly belongs to Scheduled Caste and Tribe communities. Poverty and educational deprivation co-exist notwithstanding several development programmes which are being put into operation through three tiers Panchayati Raj System. The district is a hilly area characterized by low level of literacy, with erratic distribution of rainfall, low percentage of irrigated area, unfertile nature of soil and complete absence of industrial base.

The '*khondas*' are the principal inhabitants in the districts of Kandhamal. The khondas always live in groups though their family ties are not much strong. In the family life the eldest male member acts as the guardian. The sons after their marriage get separated from their parents and live with establishment of their own. But the unmarried sons and daughters, old and incapable members live together under one roof.

In this study, most of the child labourers are girls. Fifty-four percent of the total workers belong to the age group of 12-14 years. Out of 140 child labourers 79 are educated above 7th standard. These child workers are engaged in different activities such as maidservant, fire wood collection, *khalli* stitching, agricultural labourers, chips making, household industries, etc. The result of the sample survey implies that 20 per cent of the child workers are employed as maidservants. This is followed by the activity of the child worker as hotel boy/shop boy, i.e., 13.9 per cent. Very few child workers are engaged in household industries.

Child work is often considered as part of the socialization process. Work done by children tends to be considered as "help" and not work. Work done by children, including caring for animals, woodcutting and farming activities are not valued by their parents as work.

Except the child workers employed as maid servants, all others are engaged as daily wagers. Most of the child workers declined to express their view on job satisfaction. Thirty five percent of workers expressed that they have been working for more than 8 hours per day. Remuneration is very low for them. They are employed in a walking distance from their home. In response to the size of the family most respondents said that they have a large size family. The respondents have further rejoined that they have been brought up in a family suffering from abject poverty. No one has claimed that either father or mother is a government servant. Most of the houses are thatched. Sanitation facility is very poor.

It is pointed out that in Kandhamal district not a single child labour is engaged in hazardous activities. Hence it is not a major problem but we do not agree with this analogy. There are some occupations, which although not officially classified as 'hazardous' are in fact dangerous to the child worker. In a sense, every occupation is hazardous, for it not only retards the child's growth and development but also national growth and development.

Suggestions

India has all along followed a proactive policy in the matter of tackling the problem of child labour, and always stood for constitutional, statutory and developmental measures that are required to eliminate child labour. India has ratified six ILO conventions relating to child labour and three of them as early as in the first quarter of the twentieth century. Action has already been initiated for ratification of ILO Convention No. 182 concerning prohibition and immediate Action for the Elimination of the Worst Forms of Child Labour adopted at the 87th Session of the international Labour Conference. Legislative provisions have been made in various laws to protect children from exploitation at work and to improve their working conditions. In addition, a comprehensive law namely The Child labour (Prohibition and Regulation) Act, 1986 prohibits employment of children in certain hazardous occupations / activities and regulates their employment in some other areas.

The National Policy on Child Labour was formulated in 1987, which apart from requiring enforcement of legal provisions to protect the interests of children, envisages focusing on general development programmes for the benefit of child labour, and project based on plan of action in areas of high concentration of child labour. Under the project based action plan of the policy, National Child Labour Projects (NCLP) have been set up in different areas of the country to rehabilitate child labour.

The ultimate objective of the National Child Labour Projects is to convert working children into productive and participative members of society. Considering the magnitude of the problem and paucity of resources - human, material and financial, a sequential, gradual but integrated approach has been adopted. Voluntary organizations are being financially assisted for taking up welfare projects for working children where these children are provided with non-formal education, supplementary nutrition, health care and vocational/skill training.

The Government's commitment to address the problem of child labour is reflected in the announcement made in the National 'Common Minimum Programme' of the United Progressive Alliance (UPA) Government at Center (2004). The agenda states that the aim is to ensure that no child remains illiterate, hungry or lacks medical care and that measures will be taken to eliminate child labour and protect the 'Child Rights'.

In fact the legislations enacted so far have been institutionalizing the system of child labour by making regulative provisions. There has been lukewarm response of the government in implementation of policies for combating the problem of child labour. Regarding the effective implementation of the laws we can suggest the following points.

1. The present legislation dealing with child labour is either defective or deficient. It is necessary to have a comprehensive child labour code. The law must extend its hand to the unorganized and informal sectors like agriculture, family occupation, etc.
2. It is high time to define the most confusing and complicated term 'hazardous'. It is necessary to review the present list of occupation and a detailed classification should be made about permitted 'light work' or 'non-hazardous' occupations. The child workers may be shifted from 'hazardous' to 'non-hazardous' occupations. However, they should not be driven to unprotected and unregulated where the hazard lies in the treatment of the employers though not in the nature of the job.
3. The Government must also initiate and support youth wings in all trade unions and in which child workers below 15 years of age should be allowed to take membership. The adult members in the union should take care of the welfare of these children.
4. Adequate provisions in the national legislation should be made to ensure that there should be a healthy environment in the work place of children. They should be kept out from night work and should not be allowed to carry heavy loads. They should be ensured of minimum fixed wages, limited working hours, weekly

holidays. Their physical conditions and fitness for job should be taken into account.

5. There should be a strong inspecting machinery to implement the child labour legislation. In the present system of enforcement all those inspectors are heavily burdened with different kinds of work and cannot devote sufficient time to look into the problems of child labour, safety measures adopted, payment of minimum wages, etc. Hence, it is advisable to create a separate cell of inspectors to deal with these problems. The employers, who do not comply with the required provisions, should be imposed deterrent penalties and such penalization should be widely publicized.
6. The word 'Any person' under section 16(1) of the child Labour (Prohibition and Regulation) Act, in fact does allow prosecutions by private individuals other than officials and authorities like inspectors and police officers. However, we have the opinion that voluntary organizations and trade unions can contribute a lot in implementing the law, provided their services are rightly utilized by the Government machinery. However, Government must ensure that the power, which the former may receive, should solve the purpose of defense only not the purpose of offence. This will prevent the possibility of miss-utilization of power with bad motives. Further sufficient training, orientation and certificates should be given to the voluntary organizations to enable them to enter working place without notice and to launch prosecutions.
7. There should be special children's tribunals, which may deal with the offences and atrocities against the children.
8. Commenting on the enforcement of law, the committee on child labour observed that very often-labour inspector find difficulties in collecting evidence for proper prosecution. The fact of employment of a child against law was demised both by the employer and the parents of children. To overcome this difficulty we suggest that courts should move in search of facts. The mobile courts

and tribunals can see and hear the facts without the necessity of any witnesses or documentary evidence. It achieves the ideal of dispensation of justice at the doorsteps, after catching the culprits red-handed and even they can be prosecuted on the spot summarily leaving the right of appeal to the latter. This may bring public awareness of the problem and may shake the confidence of the reckless lawbreakers, who seldom bother about the enforcement authorities and the judiciary.

Laws alone cannot change the society. Unless the economic realities of the society are changed children continue to be the victims of poverty and exploitation. Hence, laws do not operate in isolation. They function along with other socio-economic measures. Non-regulatory positive socio-economic steps are complementing to the regulatory instrument and both should operate simultaneously "like sword in one hand and shield in the other". We agree with the comment of Royal commission of labour: "we think that it is not enough merely to prohibit the employment of children, but that it is essential to adopt simultaneously positive measures to wean away child labour from industrial employment. Government owes a duty to the future generations of workers to see that childhood is not wasted in the dingy corners of factories and workshops instead of being educated in schools and brought up in nurseries and on play grounds".

Among the non-regulatory measure, two prominent instruments are: (i) free and compulsory education at least up to school leaving age, i.e., 14 years and (ii) Poverty eradication programmes to meet the economic needs of the poor.

Free and Compulsory Education

One of the important means to check the child labour problem is through free and compulsory elementary and primary education. The Government should take every effort to implement the directives enshrined in Article 45 of the constitution with regard to free and compulsory education. To achieve this following measure should be taken.

(*a*) Parents in the lower socio-economic groups are made education-conscious through intensive propaganda and publicity. They may be motivated to put their children in schools instead of labour market.

(*b*) Community crèches should be established in rural as well as in urban slum areas to relieve the children from the burden of looking after the younger brother and sisters at the cost of their schooling.

(*c*) It is necessary to take the school to the children in the case where children are working with their parents. Employers must be made responsible to see that the working children and children of working parents attend such school during stipulated time schedule,

(*d*) Part-time Non-formal education should be provided to those children employed in factories and workshops preferable during off hours. The time schedule and vocations of the schools in rural area should be adjusted to suit the requirements of the agricultural cycle with a view to facilitate child labour to take advantage of schooling facilities.

(*e*) To prevent drop-outs, the school environment and curriculum should be attractive and interesting. Measures like supply of books and uniforms at free of cost, mid-day meal and evening snacks should be introduced. Play-way method of teaching should be followed to attract the children. Even a small pocket allowance / scholarship should be given to the parent for not sending their child for economic activity.

(*f*) Government should be cautious while designing the curriculum of the school. Education system should develop confidence, creativity, courage and independence among the learners. It must give the children a strong practical base in preference to the purely theoretical. Job oriented and self-employment oriented courses should be introduced 'Learn while you earn' schemes should be made more popular.

Poverty Ameliorating Measure

1. Poverty is the main cause of child labour. Hence large scale poverty alleviation programmers should be

adopted. Effective implementation of anti-poverty programmers is an anti-dot of child labour. The provision of minimum wages must be strictly adhered to and efforts should be undertaken to achieve the goal of living wage. If the earning power of elder family members is sufficiently high, they are likely to desist from sending their children to work.

2. Cottage and small scale industries should be promoted in rural areas so as to create opportunities for the skill improvement and income augmentation for the poor communities. Special employment schemes for women and child should be so devised in and around their place of habitation to prevent their exploitation by contractors and middleman. Thus new strategies should be tailored on a micro-level basis.
3. As a concomitant to poverty eradication programme child population should be checked effectively. Hence family planning should be made compulsory and necessary infrastructure should be developed to facilitate the eligible couples to adopt a small family norm.
4. An all-out plan to stop begging, vagrancy and destitution must immediately be made. Destitute and neglected (including orphan) children also swell the ranks of child labour force. Such children may be looked after by welfare institutions and children homes. It is therefore, necessary to establish a chain of social welfare institutions to take care of these children and to create a 'National Trust' for the care of the mentally retarded and physically handicapped children.
5. Prompt measures should be taken to rehabilitate child labourers, if displaced as a result of strict enforcement of different acts / regulations.
6. NGOs must be entrusted with the responsibility of creating awareness among the people regarding child labour. They must also educate the masses that an educated youth of the family will contribute much more to the family income than uneducated child labour.

7. The exploitation of child labour is an intolerable evil, which must be eliminated as a matter of urgency. The elimination of the exploitation of child labour will require economic reforms aimed at a more equitable distribution of resources, and the active cooperation of all those concerned with the problem. Such cooperation depends on the effective mobilization of public opinion. Hence, necessary efforts may be made in this regard.
8. The State may itself promote certain industries, which are productive and non-hazardous and suitable to employ children. The main purpose of such employment is to benefit the child labour as they can learn while earning. The child workers in these industries should be provided with free food, education, vocational training, medical facility, clothes, etc. For this purpose, the Government may constitute special employment bureaus at district level. 'Searching and Placement Officers' may be appointed in all such bureaus, whose primary job is to pick up the child workers and place him in the industry with the consent of their parents. Monitoring cells may be set up at the State level to ensure that the policy is fully implemented. Thus, child may learn useful and productive work without being exploited.

The child labour problem is not an independent problem. It is a problem linked with many other problems. It is an outcome and reflection of number of socio-economic and political malfunctions. To deal with the problem, a multi-pronged attack is indispensable. Child labour issues can only be solved in a sustainable manner if an integrated approach is applied. Direct action should be coupled with local capacity building and an improvement of the legal and organizational environment. Programmes should addresses health and social services, legal protection, education, income generation and alternative employment possibilities for poverty stricken families. Public awareness raising steps are highly essential. Best results can be obtained if several actors - Government, parents & employers, work together.

Bibiography

Anandharajakumar, P., 1997, Child labour in India: Causes and Consequences, Third Concept, June, pp. 52-55.

Annual Administrative Report 1980-81 & 1981-82, DRDA Phulbani.

Benjamin. J., 1990, Child Labour: The Quest for Socio-Economic Inquiry, Third concept, December, pp. 33-36.

Burra, Neera, 1997, Child Labour in India, Oxford University Press, Delhi.

Census of India, 2001, Census Directorate, Orissa.

Child Labour: A Threat to Health and Development, Defence for Children, Geneva, 1981.

Child Labour: Targeting the Intolerable. International Labour Conference (Report VI, i)-86th Session, 1998, ILO, Geneva.

Dinesh, B.M., 1988, Economic Activities of Children, Daya Publishing House, Delhi.

District Statistical Handbook, Kandhamal, 2005, Directorate of Economic & Statistics, Orissa.

Economic Survey, 2004-05, Government of India, New Delhi.

Farooqui, V., 1993, Cruel Treatment and Abuse of Girl Child, Kapur, P., (Ed), Girl Child and Family Violence, Har Ananda Publications, p. 199.

Fyfe Alec, 1989, Child Labour, Polity Press Publications.

Jain, S.N., 1979, Child and the Law, New Delhi.

Jain, S.N., Preventive Legal measures in the Area of Child Labour, National Seminar on Child labour and the Law (Unpublished), 1982.

Jawa, R., 1999, "Female Child Labour and Poverty", Need for New Strategy to Eradicate Poverty, Gaur, K.D., (Ed), Manak Publication, New Delhi.

Jha, A., 1989, The Problem of Child labour, Third Concept, March, pp. 29.

Juyal, B.N., 1985, Child Labour and Exploitation in the Carpet Industry, Indian Social Institute, New Delhi, pp. 33.

Khare, V., 2002, Human Rights in India: Issues and Perspective, A Case Study of Child labour, Third Concept, September, pp. 31-33.

Kulshreshtha, J.C., 1978, Child Labour in India, Ashis Publishing House, New Delhi.

Kumar, B., 2000, Problems of Working Children, A.B.H. Publishing Corporation, New Delhi.

Labour Statistics in Orissa, 2004, Labour Commissioner, Government of Orissa, Bhubaneswar.

Mandelievich, Elias, 1979, Child Labour, International Labour Review, 118, 5, pp. 557-568.

Myron Weiner, 1991, The Child and the State in India: Child Labour and Education Policy in Comparative Perspective, Princeton University Press.

Nagaraj A.G., Indian Council for Child labour Welfare: The Working Child, National seminar of Employment of Children in India.

Nanjunda, D.C., 2005, Panchayats and Rural Child Labour, Third Concept, September, pp. 37-40.

Pandey, R., 1993, Street Children in Kanpur, National Labour Institute, Child labour Cell, Noida.

Panicket, R., & Nangia. P., 1992, Working and Street Children in Delhi, National Labour Institute, Child labour Cell, Noida.

Pattanaik, M., 1979, Child Labour in India: Size and Occupational Distribution, Chaturvedi, T.N. (Ed) Administration for Child Welfare, Indian Institute of Public Administration publishing, p. 136.

Peoples Union of Democracy, AIR, 1982, S.C., 1473.

Rao, R., 1998, women Workers in Beedi Industry, Social Welfare, Volume 45, Number 5, August.

Report of the Committee on Child labour (Gurupada Swamy), Ministry of Labour, Government of India, 1979.

Report of the Committee on Child Labour in India, Ministry of Labour, Government of India, 1954.

Rodgers, G., and Standing, G., 1981, Economic Roles of Children in low income Countries, International Labour Review, 120, 1.

Sahoo, U.C., 1995, Child labour in Agrarian Society, Rawat Publications, New Delhi.

Satapathy, T., 1985, Marketing Strategy in Tribal Development Planning in Orissa: An Appraisal, Orissa Economic Journal, Vol. xviii, pp. 71.

Seal, K.C., 1979: 'Children and Employment', Profile of the Child Labour in India, Barnabas, A.P., *et. al.*, (Eds), Ministry of Social Welfare, Government of India.

Sharma, B.K., *et. al.*, 1990, Child Labour and Urban Informal Sector, Deep and Deep Publications, Delhi.

Sikiligar, P.C., 1997, Evaluation of Centrally Sponsored Scheme of Boys Hostel for Schedule Castes, NIRD, Hyderabad, Unpublished Report.

Swepston, Lee, 1982, Child Labour: Its Regulations by ILO Standards and National Legislation, International Labour Review, 121, pp. 557-589.

Tripathy, S.N., 1989, Bonded Labour in India, Discovery Publishing House, New Delhi.

Tripathy, S.N, 1979, Migrant Child Labour in India, Mohit Publications, New Delhi.

Varma, A.P., & Jain, M., 1995, Trade Unions Child Labour and IPEC, National Labour Institute, Child labour Cell, Noida.

Weiner, M., 1991, The Child and the State in India, Oxford University Press.

World of Works No. 16, 1996.

World of Work No. 4, 1993.

World of Work, No. 18, 1996.

Index

L

M

N

O

P

R

S

❑❑❑